Lessons in Secular Criticism

University of
Western Sydney
Bringing knowledge to life

Thinking Out Loud: The Sydney Lectures in Philosophy and Society

These annual lectures aim to be theoretical in nature, but also to engage a general audience on questions about politics and society. The lectures are organized by the University of Western Sydney, in collaboration with ABC Radio National, the State Library of New South Wales, and Fordham University Press.

BOOK SERIES EDITOR
Dimitris Vardoulakis

LECTURE SERIES EXECUTIVE COMMITTEE
Chair: Dimitris Vardoulakis
Christopher Peterson
Joe Gelonesi
Helen Tartar

STATE LIBRARY®
NEW SOUTH WALES

(((RadioNational
abc.net.au/radionational

Lessons in Secular Criticism

STATHIS GOURGOURIS

FORDHAM UNIVERSITY PRESS

New York 2013

Library of Congress Cataloging-in-Publication Data is
available from the publisher.

Printed in the United States of America

15 14 13 5 4 3 2 1

First edition

to my nephews, Orestis and Iason,
to my son, Petros,
and to the youth of the world,
whom my generation
has failed

Contents

Preface		xi
Acknowledgments		xxiii
1.	The *Poiein* of Secular Criticism	1
2.	Detranscendentalizing the Secular	28
3.	Why I Am Not a Post-secularist	65
4.	Confronting Heteronomy	90
5.	The Void Occupied Unconcealed	120
6.	Responding to the Deregulation of the Political	145
	Index	181

Preface

In 1977, three years before his fatal accident, Roland Barthes was elected to the Chair of Literary Semiology at the Collège de France and gave the celebrated inaugural lecture that was published under the simple title *Leçon* (1978). It was a lesson in perfect Barthes fashion, on the power of a certain kind of language to resist the totalizing power that exists in the midst of all language as a social institution. He specified this as the language of literature, but he configured it broadly enough for literature to coincide with the act of writing as such or the creation of a certain textuality, as was the idiom of the day. But, remarkably, there is nothing dated in this train of thought, even if the permutations of power in today's world have significantly changed, in part by having absorbed the knowledge and language of counterpower developed by that preeminent generation of thinkers.

Barthes delivers here an inaugural lesson and, at the same time, a discourse on lesson, on the act of seeking new ideas by thinking out loud in front of a seminar audience, as have been the time-honored practices of the seminars at the Sorbonne.

His phrasing for this activity—"to dream one's research aloud" (*de rêver tout haut sa recherche*)—is uttered in full cognizance of the extraordinary privilege of acting in an institutional context that is orchestrated, strictly speaking, to operate "outside the boundaries of power"—in French simply noted as *hors pouvoir*.[1] We can, of course, raise all kinds of skeptical questions about the merit of this assertion. What institution is really ever outside the boundaries of power, and how could anyone in his or her right mind assume that some of the longest-existing, almost ancestral, institutions have survived *hors pouvoir*? And what does it mean to operate "outside the boundaries of power" while residing within the boundaries of an institution—any institution, much less a venerable institution like the Collège de France? These questions go to the heart of the contemporary discussion about higher education in the Euro-American sphere, in a historical moment shamelessly driven by the command to turn universities into corporations, while simultaneously proclaiming the social irrelevance of a humanities mode of learning in a market of quantifiable skills.

This paradoxical privilege of inhabiting the institutions of power but speaking a language *hors pouvoir* from within has been the main target of the methodical corporatization of the university in Europe and North America. In the political juncture of his day, Barthes remains unaware of this as a possibility in the future, but in retrospect he seems to be conducting a ceremony about the nature of the life of the university on the horizon of its eventual extinction. This too is part of the paradoxical privilege. It haunts our every utterance, perhaps less in the classroom, where the experimental nature of all pedagogy is palpable and real bodies with real minds and real affect shake language from its sovereignty, but surely when we seek to

1. Roland Barthes, "Inaugural Lecture, Collège de France," in *A Barthes Reader*, ed. Susan Sontag, trans. Richard Howard (New York: Hill and Wang, 1982), 458. Hereafter cited in the text. French publication as *Leçon* (Paris: Seuil, 1978).

speak against the institution, or outside it, in a public sphere desperately trying to protect itself from its own increasing abstraction. Barthes explicitly calls language "fascist," not because it represses what we say but because it compels what we say. So the wager of speaking *hors pouvoir*—of daring to think of speaking *hors pouvoir*—is how we outmaneuver this compulsion, how we speak against the language that speaks us, to use again the idiom of the day, and therefore, "to cheat with speech, to cheat speech [*tricher avec la langue, tricher la langue*]" (462).

To be accurate, this wager is less about language, simply in a linguistic sense, and more about exposing *how*—in *what* language, in what manner, with what staging—society's institutions speak on their behalf and against what threatens them, or even more precisely, on how institutions sustain their believability by rendering their adversaries unbelievable, incredible, and indeed impossible. After all, this was the mark of Barthes's maverick semiology, which, let us not forget, foregrounded society's mythographic theatricality long before discourses of performativity became current. *S/Z* was about impersonation, and its strategy of reading ultimately drew more from Brecht than from Saussure. So here, too, the handling of language is dramatic: "Because it *stages* [*met en scène*] language instead of simply using it, literature feeds knowledge into the machinery of infinite reflexivity: through writing, knowledge ceaselessly reflects on knowledge, in terms of a discourse that is no longer epistemological, but dramatic" (463–64).

This *mise en scène* destabilizes the abstract sovereignty of knowledge, as well as the concrete sovereignty of both the subject and the object of knowledge. Staging the dialectics of subject and object in this way relieves us of the instrumentality that sustains and reiterates their sovereignty. For there is no subject of knowledge that is not simultaneously an object of knowledge, and vice versa—that's what ceaseless self-reflection means. Because this dialectical image is dramatic, simultaneity can never be reduced to an epistemological collapse; it animates instead the kind of self-questioning without which no pedagogy is worthy of its name. Destabilizing the sovereignty of knowledge begins with the recognition that questioning oneself is questioning the institution that enables this process—"this enormous, almost unjust, privilege" (458)—to begin with. Barthes makes sure we recognize that the privilege of speaking "outside the boundaries of power" is in fact an instituted privilege—it does not come by fiat, by talent, or by divine inspiration. It too is the mark of a certain social-historical institution and is therefore permanently threatened by the power that has permitted us to stake out the presumptive domain of thinking outside power: "The freer such teaching, the further we must ask ourselves as to under what conditions and by what processes discourse can be disengaged from all will-to-possess [*tout vouloir-saisir*]" (459). Because no lesson is impervious to the lurking desire for power, the object of a lesson—beyond the technical dimensions of each discipline—is to place itself, its own power, and its own framework of speaking to power under question.

It should be obvious why I have taken a moment to remind us of this once celebrated but now rather neglected lesson. I chose to title this series of texts *Lessons in Secular Criticism* because I see the task of secular criticism to be putting into question the means by which knowledge is presented as sovereign, unmarked by whatever social-historical institution actually possesses it. I discuss the permutations of secular criticism at length in the texts that follow, so I will not detain us with definitions here, except to reiterate, very broadly, what I think is elementary: Namely, secular criticism is the practice of elucidating the ruse of those tacit processes that create, control, and sustain conditions of heteronomy, that is, conditions where the power of real men and women is configured to reside in some unassailable elsewhere. This practice of elucidation is quintessentially pedagogical in the way that Barthes outlines, for one learns to combat heteronomy by undoing the sovereignty of the self who conceptualizes and authorizes learning as if knowledge is other. In this very simple sense, all learning (and, of course, teaching) is, first and foremost, self-learning, autodidactic learning, according to that unavoidable paradox that knowledge can never be mastered and can never be a master, for whatever I know (in order to teach myself) is always destabilized by whatever I don't know (in order to learn) in a continuously shifting process that ends only when I die.

But there is another reason I turned to Barthes as a point of entry. Such teaching and learning, he says, take place when one can "dream one's research aloud," which, if we keep the notion rigorous, takes dreams outside their solipsistic silence into a public space where they resonate with the dreams of others. When I was presented with the honor of giving the Sydney Lectures in Philosophy and Society, I was immediately struck by the requisite stipulation of "thinking out loud," which I take here to be integral not only to how thinking is to take place but to what sort of thinking is to take place. If secular criticism is going to be worthy of its task, it must not take place in the secrecy and solitude of one's spirit but in the shared space of contentious thinking together. Secular criticism is democratic criticism, as Edward Said, who invented the notion, came to call it in his last work. In this sense, secular criticism entails the practice of a certain mode of political being.

So, although the experimental thinking that goes on in these pages is drawn from a long-term effort on my part to reconceptualize the space of the secular against both the limitations of secularism as institutional power and the new orthodoxy going by the name "post-secularism," it is explicitly dedicated to the risk of thinking out loud, of exposing the varied (and sometimes contradictory) contours of one's thought process to the public eye and ear without the benefit of the scholarly apparatus that usually safeguards academic writing. As much as is possible within the demands of a written text, all the essays retain the modalities of their having been performed as public lectures, chiefly at the State Library of New South Wales in Sydney, where they were also broadcast on Radio National of the Australian Broadcasting Corporation (ABC RN), but also on other

occasions, whether within a university framework, a public fo-
rum, or an open Internet medium. And all the essays bear the
imprint of comments, critiques, or arguments made by audiences and interlocutors on those occasions, as well as my own
thinking-out-loud responses (in instances when the conversations happened to be recorded), which is a privilege rarely
granted to any writer.

As is the essential mark of the essay as a form, each text is
composed of its own trajectory. And although there is a specific
architecture that entwines them all, there is no intended sequen-
tial argument or cumulative proposition. In musical terms, this
is perhaps a song cycle, that is, a circulation of certain motifs (or
even literally phrasings) composed on a variety of settings that
seek no particular resolution but are nonetheless self-contained
in their specific arrangements. By its very nature, thinking out
loud does not shirk from retracing already-trodden ground in
the same insistent spirit of discovering possibly overlooked traces
or improvising on a different scale material that may be thought
to be already set. Whatever is being thought out in such retracing registers itself by resonance, either with material already de-
ployed in various ways in public (whether otherwise performed
or actually published) or with a vast range of responses by read-
ers, audiences, and interlocutors, whether friendly or adversarial,
which keep this material living, pulsing, and shifting.

From this standpoint, the Sydney Lectures were an immensely fortunate event, for they came at the apex of extensive
research, teaching, publication, and performance of work on the
question of the secular that has been ongoing for more than
ten years, since the yearlong seminar at the Center for Cultural
Analysis at Rutgers, conducted by Michael Warner, and soon
after, the conversation on critical secularism in *boundary 2*,
conducted by Aamir Mufti. The work that emerged from these
collaborative occasions has already been channeled into two
nearly completed book projects, *The Perils of the One* and *Nothing Sacred*, which have been bearing *Lessons in Secular Criticism* as a subtitle. The present text, as a realization of the Sydney

Lectures, figures simultaneously as both prelude and distillation of the work contained in the other two books, forming in this respect—but really, in an entirely unexpected, accidental, way—a triptych of self-contained meditations on a problem too extensive and too slippery to be handled in one particular way and by one particular method.

In fact, in this laborious and long-term process of thinking, teaching, and writing, I discovered that the discussion of the problem of the secular—I detest the coarse general term "secularism" and, even more, the absurd nomenclature "post-secularism"—was ever more bound to questions of disciplinary knowledge and language. As the so-called secularism debates grew at furious speed and unexpected scale, I discovered that they were disproportionally consumed by, broadly speaking, a social studies methodology, with specific investments in an ethnographic conceptualization of the field of research, against a critical-skeptical practice of reading the field, which, even in its most speculative elements, characterizes the disciplinary methods of literary studies, comparative literature in particular. Hence, among other reasons, my insistence in underlining the notion of secular criticism, which emerges from literary studies and persists in this mode even in my most philosophical meditations, even when I am engaged in problems of political theory. Hence also my persistence in connecting the question of the secular to the language of *poiēsis* in its most distilled meaning, that is, the capacity of human beings to alter radically the forms and structures they inherit, which has led me, in certain instances, to inquiries of an ontological nature on the way to a political analysis beyond mere institutional structures or social-historical occurrences.

In this sense, my research into the question of the secular is inextricable from my concern with reconfiguring the conceptual terrain of radical democratic politics against a range of presumably allied competitors that run the gamut from the various permutations of liberalism to the ever more desperately fashionable Jacobin leftisms of all creeds. So, by sheer historical conjuncture, these lectures embody the lessons of the political-economic situation of the last few years: the brutal demolition of societal safeguards worldwide as a point of leveraging the scorched-earth policies of global financial capitalism. The question of the secular—the implications of what it means to encounter one's life as a worldly affair and responsibility that rests on no foundation—cannot be explored in disregard of the question of social autonomy: the implications of people refusing to consent to modes and institutions of authority that exceed them. This has become more dramatic in today's world, when various discourses of emancipation from imperialist power are advocated in theological terms. Such discourses are delineated in a stunning range of expressions: from masses of the faithful in spaces of worship or in the street confirming, in their rebellion, their obedience to external authority to media manipulators, from radio and television to print and the Internet, stoking the exclusivist cultural passageways to conformism, and to enlightened beneficiaries of disenchantment in prominent universities and think tanks who presume to be radicals. In the end, all these discourses either share or participate in safeguarding the worst of contemporary capitalism: conforming to a way of life where "leaders" (of whatever fashion, "secular" or "religious") conduct politics on your behalf while you settle for whatever is the conventional expectation of a "good life," with the only concern being how to enhance it.

The December 2008 events in Greece, chiefly in Athens but also in many other cities around the country, which signaled a spontaneous insurrection of the country's youth (including immigrant youth), unplanned and unmanaged, have been a watershed for me.[2] It was the first response to the cost of a way

---

2. Hence my decision to frame this book in a series of epigraphs that emerged from the streets during those days. I have translated these from the Greek collection of images and photographs *Unrest [Ανησυχία]: An Account of the Spontaneous in December 2008,* ed. Alexandros Kyriakopoulos and Efthymios Gourgouris (Athens: Kastaniotis, 2009).

of life exemplified by the crisis of Western capitalism, signaled by the U.S. banking collapse of the same year. Of course, they occurred not because any one in Greece understood the magnitude of the historical moment, which was soon to spread to the de facto disintegration of the Eurozone, but because, in an utterly visceral and inconfigurable way, young Greeks had sensed with horror that the future of their life had been sold down the river. The insurrection was fueled by extraordinary rage, not only against the obvious avatars of commodification but also against all legitimacy: civil, social, political, cultural. Hence the unleashed fury of destruction. The broad phenomenon of assembly movements in public spaces that emerged as the insidious realities of financial capitalism were unconcealed was the next step, the other side, in the expression of this fury—not its sublimation but its reorientation into a radical democratic politics. However, the fury and the rage remain, because, for one thing, democracy has not been founded without them since the days of Sophocles, but also because the legitimacy of political institutions that escorted the rampage of financial capitalism has been utterly discredited.

The economic crisis is really a crisis of the political. Perhaps that is always the case, but that is a theoretical discussion, and we miss the point. The current crisis of the political is liberating economic forces of unprecedented and uncontrollable magnitude. Capital is endemically incapable of self-regulation. So, ironically, some of its greatest gains have been the result of political intervention, occasionally even by its quintessential enemies, the workers movement. But all these gains came with substantial cost, which was duly deemed transferrable to hapless others in an ever-expanding geography of victims. Because this transferability is shrinking by the speed of its own expansion, the political forces of masses of people expressing themselves carry high risk; hence access to the political is increasingly impeded, either by overt repression or by covert manipulation and manufacturing of consent, so that economic forces can run unregulated. Part of this manipulation takes place via political-theological discourses, some of them quite explicit and extensive, so that a meditation on the problem of the secular—a meditation that would seek to reconfigure the language of the secular away from its institutionalized secularism—is not merely a matter of scholarship. It is a political matter. The various political theologies that are currently animating broad constituencies of political actors in many parts of the world not only feed on their constitutive exclusionism, thereby disenfranchising large masses of people, but also buttress sovereignties (from national state apparatuses to civic or cultural institutions) that continue to deprive people of their freedom to act on their own behalf. Whatever the inadequacies of institutionalized secularism are—and they are many—it seems self-evident to me that only a secular social space can handle the conflicts of social differentiation and enable a new radical democratic politics to flourish.

My musings in these texts take place in confrontation with this task. Just as I could never claim to speak "outside the boundaries of power" from within the institution, I am perfectly cognizant, to return to Barthes for a moment, of how "power seizes upon the pleasure of writing as it seizes upon all pleasure, to manipulate it and to make of it a product that is gregarious and non-perverse . . . , to turn it into militants and soldiers for its own profit" (468). It is therefore imperative, he argues, to shift ground, to shift one's own ground [*se déplacer*], which means "to go where you were not expected, or more radically, to *abjure* what you have written (but not necessarily what you have thought), when gregarious power uses and subjugates it" (468). To think in secular terms means to accept—Barthes would even say to seek—a shifting ground in your modes of knowledge so, if your language cannot entirely resist being appropriated by the institution, it can perhaps discredit this appropriation. Hence, perhaps, the sometimes unrealistic dimensions of this writing. Hence, also, the propensity to consider the ruses of reality from the standpoint of thinking about what Foucault used to call "unrealized instances"—folds that history or knowledge has yet to open, which are nonetheless ever persistently in play, haunting and provoking our thinking out loud in response to a contemporary reality ever driven to secrecy and to silence behind the continuous noise machine of media technologies.

Galaxidi and New York, August–September 2012

Acknowledgments

This book is composed chiefly on the basis of Thinking Out Loud: The Sydney Lectures in Philosophy and Society, which I presented on May 21–25, 2012, at the State Library of New South Wales. The lectures were sponsored by the University of Western Sydney in collaboration with the State Library of New South Wales, the Australian Broadcasting Corporation (which broadcast the lectures on Radio National), and Fordham University Press, which is the publisher of the Sydney Lectures series.

My profound gratitude goes to Dimitris Vardoulakis, who is the ingenious composer and orchestrator of this extraordinary yearly event and whose friendship and intellectual companionship I treasure in ways I cannot express in words. The privilege of presenting my work in Sydney in this context was enhanced by an unforgettable intellectual experience of practically non-stop encounters in the course of two weeks. A great part of these discussions and arguments found its way into the written material, and a lot more is certain to be included in future writings. For this good fortune, I am especially grateful to Melinda

Cooper, Farid Y. Farid, Joel Graham, John Hadley, Gail Jones, Nicholas Kompridis, Alex Ling, Chris Peterson, Amanda Third, Anthony Uhlmann, Jess Whyte, and above all the late Alan Saunders, on whose legendary radio show *The Philosopher's Zone* I had the sad honor of being the last guest.

The work that led to the Sydney Lectures has been conceived and conducted over a number of years, and earlier stages of it have been presented in various contexts of publication and performance. For their generosity in supporting and hosting the part of my work that specifically found its way into this publication, I wish to thank Jonathan Van Antwerpen for including me in the discussions of *The Immanent Frame* from the outset; Dilip Parameshwar Gaonkar for inviting me to publish the earliest instance of "Detranscendentalizing the Secular" and my subsequent exchange with Saba Mahmood in the pages of *Public Culture*; Ali Behdad and Dominick Thomas for soliciting my contribution to their *Companion to Comparative Literature*; Nasir Yousafzai Khan for his unwavering hospitality in *Al Jazeera*; Paul Bové and the *boundary 2* Editorial Collective for underwriting the collaborative engagement of the question "Why I am not a post-secularist" and for a great deal more; Vicky Unruh and Simon Gikandi for asking me to share my views on the deregulation of the political in the pages of *PMLA*; Andrew Arato and *Constellations* for including me in the memorial colloquium on Claude Lefort at the New School of Social Research; Sophie Klimis and Philippe Caumières for inviting me to participate in the *Journées Castoriadis* in Brussels in May 2011.

No thinking worthy of its name ever happens in the echo chamber of one's own mind. Although I bear sole responsibility for any errors and excesses of this writing, I cannot claim proprietory knowledge of its innovations. My learning has been informed by numerous friends and adversaries on countless occasions, but specifically regarding this material, I wish to express gratitude to Aamir Mufti, who was the first to break through the problem of secularism, more than a decade ago, by dismantling facile or fashionable alternatives and by raising the stakes of what is immanently critical in the secular—to the pleasure of our ongoing thinking together I owe more than I can ever acknowledge; Gil Anidjar, whose tireless argument has saved me from many pitfalls and continues to elucidate the tacitly unexamined corners of my thought; Andreas Kalyvas, whose agonistic companionship is a never-ending source of radical discovery and wondrous invention; and Martin Harries, in whose wry wisdom and refined sense of reading my mind finds welcome and playful rest.

I must also express deserved gratitude to friends who, sometimes explicitly and precisely, other times inadvertently and unwittingly, have opened up new avenues in my thinking, or enabled me to evade the perils of my hardheadedness, or, even more, liberated my spirit from the treadmill of inertia that tends to take over such decade-long research projects. In this respect, I am indebted to Sadia Abbas, Emily Apter, Athena Athanasiou, Etienne Balibar, Aristides Baltas, Dušan Bjelić, Jean Cohen, Arne de Boever, Victoria de Grazia, Mehmet Dosemeci, Costas Douzinas, Simon During, Bernard Flynn, Carlos Forment, Eleanor Kaufman, Virginia Jackson, Ronald Judy, Vassilis Lambropoulos, Thomas B. Lemann, Antonis Liakos, Michael Löwy, Saloni Mathur, Kirstie McClure, Meredith McGill, Edward Mitchell, Andrew Parker, Yopie Prins, Arvind Rajagopol, Anupama Rao, Kriss Ravetto, Bruce Robbins, Fotini Tsalikoglou, Constantine Tsoukalas, Nadia Urbinati, Eleni Varikas, Anthony Vidler, Michael Warner, Joel Whitebook, and Jim Wiltgen. To this list no doubt belong those select students at Columbia and UCLA who, during the past decade, have unsparingly taught me to listen and to rethink; their youthful intellectual unrest has ensured that teaching is, first and foremost, learning.

But in the end, when all is said and counted, nothing of what I do that makes books like this happen can be measured. Writing has always been tantamount to living for me, which is to say that living is what writing is all about. To this realization

I could never remain honest and true if it were not for the sense of freedom that comes from sharing the sun-drenched love of every mortal day with Neni Panourgia, my life's companion, and our son, Petros, who reminds us daily that living is an adventure to be embraced with boundless spirit.

Dear God, I can handle the wolves, but please save me from the sheep
Our only homeland is our childhood
In the world of the bosses we are all foreign workers
We ask for nothing because we want it all
We who have known no playgrounds learned early on to play in the streets
We break shop windows not because life is costly but because our comforts conceal life's real cost
We represent a reality we are trying to forget
We are an image from the future
Stop the tear gas! WE weep on our own
I don't want to work, I need time for NOTHING
Nothing less than everything
Make the impossible happen. Move the lines of the probable.
Fuck May '68. Fight Now.
PARADISE has been destroyed. It's time for some to go to HELL.
The desire to be normal produces monsters
Philosophy in the streets is poetry on the barricades
War expressed in poetry is poetry lived as war
Death is overcome by living
History is written with stones
Christmas is finished. The Virgin had an abortion.
December was not a response. It was a question.

Slogans from the December 2008 youth insurrection
in Athens and other Greek cities

ONE

The *Poiein* of Secular Criticism

My initial interest here, before I elaborate on the capacity of the notion in question, is to situate the advent of secular criticism, not in the broad and nebulous sphere of the secularism debates (and the so-called post-secular universe that underlies them), but in the precise historical sphere to which it belongs. Hence I present a brief retrospective account of certain theoretical strains in the trajectory of comparative literature as an epistemic field.

The best recent arguments to reconsider our understanding of comparative literature as a discipline and mode of thinking—two trenchant examples are Gayatri Chakravorty Spivak's *Death of a Discipline* (2003) and Emily Apter's *The Translation Zone* (2006)—emerge from the core experience of so-called high theory and carry within them the historical range of its permutations, including voluminous "posts" and "antis," attempted turns and counterturns, and proclaimed ends and terminations. Both Spivak and Apter, in terms that ultimately do not diverge, demand that we remain focused on the interminable question of language, which, in defiance of the prison house of philosophy (the hegemony of conceptual analysis), continues to reinforce the fact that literature's trajectory across historical, geographic, economic, and technological terrains still remains unpredictable and unmasterable, even if it is fluid and all-pervasive. Hence the attention of both works to translation as the most evocative trope of literature's unique way of encountering (and occasionally forging) conditions toward planetarity.

Such work springs from theory and remains rigorously theoretical, steadily resisting those quarters in the academy (but also in the educated public sphere) that hastened to proclaim, with evident self-satisfaction, the death of theory and all its malicious consequences. The antitheoretical strain that has come into full force in the past decade permeates all disciplines, especially historical and political studies, but it has registered with particular vehemence in literary studies itself, no doubt because of the well-honed perception that theory was dangerous to literature and that, as a result, literary studies have been suffering for some time from the incapacity to remain relevant to the contemporary conditions of knowledge production. A succinct exposition of this perspective can be found in Marjorie Perloff's Modern Language Association presidential address a few years ago.[1]

From a certain standpoint, Perloff's lament that literary study has been relegated to a secondary position in the research framework of higher education in the United States does indeed have merit. This standpoint, however, rests on a kind of retrospective (so as not to say outright, nostalgic) comparison of today's institutional parameters with an era in which literary study enjoyed an enviable autonomy, a self-authorization that went so far as to demarcate not merely the practice of the study of literature (the discipline of literary criticism) but even what we might call a literary way of thinking. This was how the in-

---

1. Marjorie Perloff, "Presidential Address 2006: It Must Change," *PMLA* 122 (2007): 652–62.

stitution of theory took hold in American universities, and it is elementary to recall that many other disciplines, principally in the social sciences but also in the arts, conceded to literary studies the vanguard of the methodological and epistemological reconfigurations of their own disciplinary boundaries. Anthropologists, historians, film critics, or art historians who suddenly acceded to the position of theorist came to regard literary studies as an inventory for whatever new terms or concepts they deemed necessary in unsettling their own disciplinary givens. In this peculiar way, the advent of interdisciplinarity in the American academy took place, historically, from within the disciplinary parameters of literary studies, indeed, as an excess of literary studies.[2] Whoever experienced this period firsthand (I would date it from the late 1970s to about 1990) should remember that this excessive condition bore—as the notion itself would have it—something ecstatic.

There is obviously much to be said about the advent of this new institution—what was later codified as "the theory turn"— but its heterogeneity was perhaps its most radical element. The achievement of a certain critical perspective that dismantles the self-certainty of hitherto-unassailable structures characterizes this shift above and beyond any of the particulars. Let us recall, first, that from the outset this shift was tied to practices of multiple learning, and, second—these two moments are linked—it was precipitated by extraordinary experimentation. Contrary to what the enemies of theory have always been arguing, the experience of theory breaking out in American universities was not driven by concepts but by practices. And although it is true that voluminous names emerged, which, by becoming

2. Let us note that this is the primary academic space worldwide where one can make the claim of interdisciplinarity being a reality—despite the fact that this claim is, in practice, still overstated and overestimated—because this geographic site, the heart of the imperial beast, has served as the focal point of a worldly intelligentsia in the making, expatriate and homeless at the core.

fashionable, began to be traded as golden concepts, both the speed with which these names were overwritten by others and the ultimate confusion that was produced when anyone tried to work on that basis alone—that is, by reproducing the conceptual terrain suggested by the newest hot theory term etc.— testify to what I am suggesting. The turn to theory was a fecund period of experimental practices of radical interrogation, subversion of established modes of interpretation, daring cognitive ingenuity, and irreverent performativity. It mobilized groundbreaking opportunities for collective learning, often by relentless argument and counterargument. It was thus profoundly political, if nothing else in the barest sense of exposing unquestioned domains in the structures of power (of both domination and liberation) and producing new modes of consciousness about what constitutes authority and agency, even when (or perhaps especially when) the notions of "author" and "agent" were attacked head on.

Let us also recall how quickly and vastly this terrain of thought and argument was internationalized, long before discussions of globalization came to the forefront in economics journals and market-research media. The advent of interdisciplinarity, in this respect, was hardly aberrant or forced. On the contrary, it was the inevitable outcome of this excessive interrogation of boundaries of all kinds—not merely epistemological but also historiographical, geographic, and cultural (eventually exported to reconfigurations of lifestyle in the larger public sphere)—that emerged out of the academic parameters of literary studies, comparative literature in particular. Our field became a kind of broker of exchanges between specific disciplinary languages as they tried to reconfigure themselves in order to participate in the opening up of new domains of interrogation and make interdisciplinary dialogue possible. Graduate studies in comparative literature in the 1980s posed the formidable challenge of mastering both the canonical knowledge of literary criticism and literary history and the rapidly emerging and proliferating new languages of theory that opened paths to other disciplines. The work was double not in quantity (because, quantitatively, it was tenfold) but in orientation: the learning of tradition and also the learning of dismantling tradition, simultaneously and polemically conducted. In this sense it was indeed excessive. This excessive element came back to haunt the literary studies world, rebounding against it as an indication of alleged undisciplinarity: lack of rigor, epistemological falsity, disingenuous methodology, contrived inquiry, etc.[3]

In this sense, I do understand that it is not easy to grant genuineness to this condition of excess I am describing, although the allegations about its consequences are themselves motivated by evident *ressentiment* on the part of traditional disciplinarity. Certainly, for a period of a decade or more, since 1990, the micro-identitarian shift within theory did precipitate conditions of failed self-interrogation, especially regarding the profound paradoxes of the new disciplinary parameters that emerged out of the practice of interdisciplinarity. As a result, literary studies (but, I would argue, other disciplines as well) did suffer from a

---

3. It has become conventional to impute these characterizations more to cultural studies than to any other field designation within literary studies. It is worth remembering that Cultural Studies emerged primarily in English departments, less in Comparative Literature, arguably because, given that its object was essentially an assessment of contemporary culture (especially in relation to tendencies emerging from media and technology dimensions), it tended to be primarily Anglophone and even more particularly Americanist, since we are talking about a phenomenon in American universities. (Cultural Studies emerging from the University of Birmingham in late 1960s England is a whole different matter.) Because, for this reason, Cultural Studies was overwhelmingly presentist in its meteoric rise, the methodological parameters were forged with little or no historical, geographic, or even linguistic breadth; hence the imputation of "undisciplinarity." Although Cultural Studies has had an equally meteoric fall from fashion, or perhaps because of that, it has more recently developed some of its most interesting and valuable aspects as it has begun to embrace historical and geographic studies.

certain carelessness, perhaps even arrogance—one is a symptom of the other—that fostered further abandonment of self-
interrogation for the comfort of identity politics. In other
words, the condition is not external but self-induced.

The difference is decisive precisely where it matters most:
on the question of how to assert the different (and differential) epistemologies of a literary way of thinking—or for my
purposes, more precisely: the cognitive powers of the poetic
element itself.[4] My experience does not agree with Perloff's
description of the field. This is not to say that what she describes does not exist; it is to say that what she describes is not
entirely accurate. For one thing, if interdisciplinarity is indeed (and that is a big "if") the modus operandi of graduate
study in literature, the job market continues to punish interdisciplinary work. This often drives us, as advisers, to curtail
our students' complex aspirations and imaginations. We do
it out of a sense of responsibility, no doubt—we want them
to get jobs—but I wonder whether we should rethink our responsibility and apply pressure instead against the institutional status quo and toward creating the kinds of jobs that
demand and reward interdisciplinarity and not so-called
expertise.

So as not to be misunderstood, I repeat that interdisciplinarity requires, by definition, the double work of engaging the
canonical and the modes of interrogating it. Interdisciplinary
training is, first, disciplinary training. It means to take the disciplinary logic to its limit in order precisely to interrogate the
construction of the limit. It is thus a transformation of this
construction—yes, a deconstruction, if you will, so long as the

4. This is the claim I explore broadly in *Does Literature Think?* (Stanford,
Calif.: Stanford University Press, 2003), and specifically, as far as poetry is
concerned, in "Communism and Poetry," *Gramma* 8 (2000): 43–54, and "The
Lyric in Exile: Meditations on the *Hollywood Songbook*," *Qui Parle* 14, no. 2
(Fall 2004): 145–76.

(inter)disciplinarity of deconstruction itself is never reducible
to its canon.

———————

Perloff does not account for the phases of this historical trajectory and thereby misses a crucial way out of the quandary she
indexes in the present. Her argument rests on a reconfiguration
of something archaic: "Whatever the 'inter' . . . , there is one
discipline that is conspicuously absent, and that discipline is
what the Greeks called Poētikē, the discipline of Poetics." But
this reconfiguration remains archaic for two reasons: First, she
does not inquire whether poetics might be conducted nowadays in an entirely different language, which, at first glance,
may seem to have nothing to do with poetry as such; this itself
could be or become the work of literary theory or even poetic
thinking. Second—and this is symptomatic of the first—
Perloff's view of *poiētikē* might be in fact narrowly conceived,
even within the terms of its ancient usage, to refer substantively
to a skill, such as rhetoric, let us say. I would counter the substantive name of a skill (*poiētikē*) with the infinitive verb of a
practice (*poiein*), whose precise skills are voluminous and indefinite, never exhausted by the skill of crafting verses, and indeed
never immune to the transformational process of the practice.
This practice is, of course, an art, but an art that exceeds *ars
poetica* conventionally understood.

The range of *poiein* includes not merely the art of making
but the art of forming (thereby, within the domain of history,
transforming). The poet as *homo faber* is the outcome of a
modernist aspiration to shake off the sublime burden of the
romantic artist; both notions are themselves historical mark-
ings of modernity, no more, no less. The most ancient notion of
poiein, present in Homer—even if he was not an arbiter of this
ambiguity between forming and making—pertains primarily
to working on matter, shape, or form and only secondarily to
abstraction, whereby it might suggest availing or producing
forms. It is interesting to note that in strict etymology, the root

reference of creativity (*dēmiourgia*) bears a sort of communal instrumentalism. As opposed to a *poiētēs*, who encounters form as object, a *dēmiourgos* is one whose work derives its primary meaning from the public sphere, as the word itself shows: *dēmos* + *ergon*. This *ergon* covers a range of action: a *dēmiourgos* can be a seer as much as a doctor.

Arguably because of the Christian investment in the notion of creation out of the absolute, but no doubt also because of the epistemological permutations of Platonism from the Hellenistic era onward, the referential framework that comes to measure the genius of a poet is drawn not from *poiēsis* but from *dēmiourgia*. In Plato, although in *Timaeus* the notions are intertwined, one might say that a *dēmiourgos* is still in effect a worker (in *The Apology* specifically coded as an artisan) who commits an *ergon*, even if this *ergon* is the universe itself, while the poet is a shaper who shapes forms. But for Plato, shaping forms is, in the last instance, inevitably misshaping, de-forming, hence his alarm about the poet as a shaper who transforms morals—essentially a political, not an ethical, act that leaves no place for the poet but exile from the city. Plato's concern is warranted from the standpoint of what will become the philosophical (and later, theological) desire to harness an unalterable, inalienable truth. This is because shaping is always altering, and thus to form is always to *transform*, conceived, in a materialist way, as the process of bringing otherness to bear on the world, as opposed to receiving otherness as external authority. In this respect, inherent in *poiein* is also an element of destruction, and there is no external guarantee that would absolve any *poiēsis* of the destructive elements of the alteration it performs.

The modern point of view sustains this creative/destructive action in *poiein*, despite the fact that *dēmiourgein* is the verb that, in its Latin derivation (*creatio*), has taken over the range of signification. The struggle between what we can abusively call "private" and "public" poetics has not resolved, historically, the social demands posed by the idea of the poet as a shaper of forms.

The force of Plato's political prejudice has been astonishingly long lasting and crucial in the formation of modernity. Discussions of the Platonic dimensions of *poiēsis* often restrict themselves to its central invocation in the *Symposium*, where the notion is infused with various permutations of Eros. There too, however, the ultimate power of *poiēsis* consists not in the shaping of form or even the erotic creation of life but in the transformation of the soul by virtue of philosophical practice. In the usurpation of *poiēsis*, philosophy defeats poetry yet again. Since then, in the Western tradition, the transformative power of *poiein*, both as a social-imaginary but also as an artistic (poetic, strictly speaking) force, is consistently underplayed in favor of a certain analytic relation to knowledge, a philosophical *scientia* that, having fully engaged the permutations of *technē*, has come to form the backbone of the pseudorationality that animates the instrumental logic of capitalist modernity. I say this because poetry continues to remain intransigent and socially significant in largely precapitalist modes of life, even while capitalist logic is raging infrastructurally (economically, technologically, culturally, and even politically in some cases) at an extraordinary speed and scale.[5]

It is therefore no surprise that in the long procession of Western thought, whereby the quarrel between poetry and philosophy is relentlessly conducted, the advocates of *poiēsis* as material (trans)formation are those who resist the seductions of Platonism and its derivatives. Few, however, explicitly name *poiēsis* as such to be the matrix of their philosophical pursuit. One such thinker is surely Giambattista Vico, whose *Scienzia nuova* (1725) extends the Renaissance rendition of *poiēsis* beyond the task of *imitatio naturae* and indeed inaugurates thinking of

5. For an exemplary discussion of the dialectical range of this specific problem, see Aamir Mufti, "Faiz Ahmed Faiz: Towards a Lyric History of India," in his *Enlightenment in the Colony: The Jewish Question and the Crisis of Postcolonial Culture* (Princeton: Princeton University Press, 2007), 210–43.

history as a poetic project. Although it is difficult to pinpoint
Vico's direct philosophical descendants, in retrospect a vast
trajectory of strains of thought either in avant-garde poetics
(from the nineteenth century on) or political aesthetics (especially heterodox tendencies unfolding out of Hegelian Marxism),
and explicitly the thought of Edward Said, engage themselves
with similar views of history as the force of *poiein*.

This force resonates in discourses of modernity, both aes-
thetic and political. An entire society can be said to engage in
poiein in its radical moments of self-determination. In this respect, *poiein* includes (or is entwined with) a noninstrumental-
ist notion of *prattein* precisely so as to counter the permutations
of *technē* as the primary agent in the production of knowledge
and the making of history.[6] The most profound meaning of
this entwinement consists in being attuned to the elusive de-
tails of history in the making, which need not be understood in
any sort of Heideggerian sense. But the poet cannot be equated
with the historian, even when a poem is indeed a bona fide historical document, a text that produces actual historical knowledge. Even if we accept (as I do) that the most precise historical
writing must, at some level, be poetic, there is no equation between, say, *historein* and *poiein* because even the most poetic
historical writing, the writing that does indeed produce the
past, does not (as it should not) obliterate the narrative frame
of deciphering already-established ways of the world. And although, surely, poetry does also narrate, the force of *poiein*
pertains to a radical sense of the present as something, if not
quite boundless, then indeterminately bounded. When I link
poiein to history in the making, I understand it precisely as
shaping matter into form in such a way that the form itself be-

6. An admirable treatment of this entire range of questions, both philosophically and historically, is Sophie Klimis's "La musicalité sémantique du
penser-poème grec: Pour une eidétique du prattein-poiein dans le langage," in
Castoriadis et les Grecs, a special issue of, *Cahiers Castoriadis* vol. 5 (Brussels:
Publications de Facultés Universitaires Saint-Louis, 2010), 173–243.

comes the cipher for the utterly elusive meaning of its own (trans)formation. [7]

This shaping does not really have a precise temporality; hence traditional methods of historiography cannot grasp it. Its working is a perpetual reworking, a thorough reworking, that would not spare even itself as an object of that work. (The clichéd notion of a poem always being at work on itself, on making itself into a poem, should be understood here as an elemental force of *poiein*.) The duration of shaping matter into form, as Henri Bergson would have it, occurs in (or as) a radical present. This is a paradoxical condition, but that is why its boundaries exceed the capacity of both narration and symbolization (indeed, discipline) and can be considered graspable only in a performative vein. The energy of *poiein* is dramatic: Literally, to form is to make form happen, to change form (including one's own). It is an infinitive force, in a strange way an attribute of the infinite, yet not pertaining to space but to action in space—a force that forms and yet, grammatically, bears language's many forms. The political substance of *poiein* is thus not signified just by its constitutively transformative power, which would be a mere abstraction, but by the fact that in its ancient meaning, it pertains to humanity's immanent (even if perpetually self-altering) encounter with the world.

———

On such terms of worldly encounter and as an extension of arguing for a disciplinary deconstruction of the limit of discipline—this, I believe, is essential to the project of comparative literature, the requisite work of which is quintessentially *poiētic*—let me now turn to the notion whose particular

---

7. There is, in this respect, something akin to Vico here, whose notion of *sapienza poetica* meant to distinguish historical knowledge as the human capacity to make knowledge rather than to chronicle the event. This understanding of Vico is, of course, omnipresent in Edward Said's thought from *Beginnings* onward, but see indicatively his *Humanism and Democratic Criticism* (New York: Columbia University Press, 2003), 11–13.

poiein I am keen on examining. Secular criticism did emerge from the core of those polemics over theory I mentioned at the outset. The name belongs, as is well known, to Edward Said, and although it appears early on in the essay that introduces *The World, the Text, and the Critic* (1983), it can never be said to have had the benefit of unequivocal definition. Instead of a definition of a concept, Said provides multifarious descriptions of a task, which may include conceptual attitudes (without, however, providing a safeguard in a concept) but mostly pertain to certain practices of thinking and writing, foremost among which is the essay as a form. With regard to the mode of knowledge it mobilizes, the task of secular criticism, according to Said, is explicitly literary. This is a crucial thing to remember both in light of the preceding discussion and in light of much of the newly crafted terrain around issues of secularism, to which—skewed as it is by dominant philosophical or cultural-ethnographic modes of analysis—the methodological and epistemological horizon of literary studies remains incomprehensible.

Indeed, here I must confess something that may sound naïve, but I feel that it needs to be said. In recent years, I often found myself saying, in conversations with friends or in public, something to the effect that I have been trying to rethink the notion of secular criticism that Edward Said initially put forth early in his work but never actually defined, although he practiced it throughout his life, and so on. Well, I've come to realize that what has burdened me about this account, the thing I've always had to defend but never had an answer for, is the phrase "he never really defined." I cannot say anything about Said's reasons or intentions for not in fact defining, at least in a satisfactory way, what he meant by secular criticism. I don't actually know whether he really thought about it this way, whether these *Orientalism*-era concerns really mattered to him more than a whole lot of others. The question is, of course, irrelevant. The fact—and I am embarrassed to have realized it so late—is that secular criticism cannot be defined. It is not a

philosophical concept that bears the weight of an *archē*, a primary principle, upon which a hypothesis may credibly rest or
out of which a set of commands may be issued. It is not a principle at all, in the sense that whatever domain it stakes out can
never be delimited a priori, which is to say just as well that
whatever the limits of this domain are, they are themselves
the conduits of interrogation. In this respect, secular criticism
is not a theory but a practice—an experimental, often interrogative practice, alert to contingencies and skeptical toward
whatever pretends to escape the worldly. Incidentally, there is a
co-incidence here between interrogation and imagination, on
which hinges whatever path we choose to take in order to evaluate the *poiein* of secular criticism.

Thus there can never be a theory of secular criticism, which
is not to say that secular criticism does not engage in theoretical problems or indeed produce theories. To provide a defini-
tional framework of secular criticism as theory would mean to
set external and a priori rules for what would be secular and
what would be critical about it, and this would defeat the intel-
ligence of the practice on both grounds. This is a crucial error
in Talal Asad's recent attempt to define secular criticism against
and away from Said's consideration. I am referring to a short
text called "Historical Notes on the Idea of Secular Criticism"
that goes to some lengths and with subtle cunning to disorient
the discussion about secular criticism so much as to declare it a
"modern theology."[8]

---

8. This text was posted on the Immanent Frame website and went un-
commented in its specifics. (See http://blogs.ssrc.org/tif/2008/01/25/historical
-notes-on-the-idea-of-secular-criticism/.) It was subsequently incorporated
intact as a section of Asad's "Free Speech, Blasphemy, and Secular Criticism"
in the volume *Is Critique Secular? Blasphemy, Injury, and Free Speech* (Berkeley,
Calif.: Townsend Center for the Humanities, 2009), 20–63. I treat the essay
as a whole elsewhere. Here I focus specifically on this earlier fragment, but for
facility's sake I refer to the pagination from the full essay. Page references are
cited in the text.

I have already argued against what I see as a self-serving equation between the secular and the theological, increasingly championed as a key (and new) theoretical juncture or, worse yet (as far as I am concerned), as a radical political gesture. No doubt, there is a genuine debate on this issue, and the ire I have received testifies to it.[9] I confess that I am still astonished by the extraordinary identification—so as not to politicize it overtly by calling it an alliance—between, on the one hand, exceedingly and dangerously reactionary Christian antisecular attitudes on a mass scale in American society and, on the other hand, a rapidly increasing number of academics in American universities who become, rather indiscriminately, animated with antipathy to whatever is signified by whatever means as secular. That many of these academics are also considered radical anticolonial and anti-imperialist thinkers makes this convergence exceedingly puzzling and indeed worrisome. My own sense is that the tremendous hegemony of identity politics, as it developed out of the mid-1980s, still operates as a giant magnet of both ideological certainty and uninterrogated affect over the modes of thinking in these circles. I am not astonished by this ideological persistence, but I am astonished by the lack of radical political imagination, especially when the historical times demand it.

Against this newly achieved comfort, I have proposed that one of the key tropes of secular criticism is to detranscendentalize the secular, which I take to be a necessary task so as not to get trapped in the simple equation between the secular and the theological. Indeed, the only possible equation that can be conceived to exist between secularism and religion—the corresponding institutional matrix for the two substantives—is that they produce heteronomous politics. This is why it is an error to ignore the difference between secularism and secular

9. See specifically my exchange with Saba Mahmood, initially conducted in the Immanent Frame website and reproduced in *Public Culture* 20, no. 3 (Fall 2008): 437–65.

criticism, and Talal Asad reproduces this error unequivocally. The two terms cannot be equated because secularism is one of the objects taken to task—the task of interrogation and critique—by secular criticism. Hence the really troublesome term here is "critique."[10]

The root term of "critique," the Greek *krisis*, carries a rather instructive multivalence. At the primary level of meaning, it pertains to the practice of distinction and the choice involved—in other words, the decision to pronounce difference or even the decision to differ, to dispute. In this basic sense, *krisis* is always a political act. In legal or philosophical usage, it is thus linked to judgment and indeed to the fact that judgment cannot be neutral (which we still see nowadays in the commonplace negative meaning of critique as rejection). In this way, *krisis*, as judgment, distinguishes and exposes an injustice. As an extension of this meaning, we also find in the ancient usage the notion of outcome, of finality—again in the sense of the finality of decision.

Incidentally, in her insightful response to Talal Asad in the dialogue *Is Critique Secular?*, Judith Butler insists on excising the dimension of judgment from critique, a gesture she identifies as quintessentially Kantian: "Even in Kant, it is important to note that critique is not precisely a judgment, but an inquiry

10. I forgo here the question of difference between criticism and critique, for it would require a broad tangent. There may indeed be a difference. Paul Bové in his *Poetry against Torture* (Hong Kong: Hong Kong University Press, 2008) argues in favor of criticism as historical practice and against critique as philosophical speculation. Talal Asad, in the text discussed here, situates the emergence of critique as a practice of theological interpretation (Reformation hermeneutics), which then serves as the platform for Kantian rationalist metaphysics, ultimately to claim that the two terms occupy a similar Christian/secularist terrain. No doubt, a rather precise genealogy for how the two terms ("critique" and "criticism") form different significations in the various European languages in which they come into use is warranted. However, the Greek significational framework that underlies them both cannot be gotten around.

into the conditions that make judgment possible. That inquiry is, and must be, separate from judgment itself. . . . Following Kant, critique is prior to judgment."[11] I find this position puzzling because no evaluation of conditions of possibility—since inquiry entails, at some level, an evaluation of some kind—can be enacted without judgment. Conditions of possibility do not exist intact in some objective sphere to be discovered. They are judged to be conditions of possibility—they become possible as conditions of possibility—in the situation of inquiry and evaluation, and therefore, they can be revised or disputed. Butler certainly knows this and has shown it in exemplary ways throughout her work. I am not sure why she directs her discourse in this way here. Moreover, no inquiry/evaluation, and therefore judgment, can be devoid of politics. This Butler also knows, as evidenced by a comment later in her text that seems to contradict the one above: "To enter into political action surely requires some kind of judgment about what is the case, and what should be the case" (124). No doubt – but also, isn't this ("what is the case and what should be the case") a description of evaluation?

Whatever might be the modern weight of ethical language on the meaning of critique, its groundwork remains political. Decisions have to be made, and to make them is to be accountable for them, to be judged on their basis. This inevitably happens in—indeed, it creates—a field of contention. Even if the act of differing is addressed to an array of neutral objects, it can never be disengaged from the subject position; the one who differentiates is also the one who differs. Considering that no subject position in the ancient Greek world was conceivable outside the *polis*, the work of the discerning mind, the mind that makes and acts on a decision, would have to be engaged in

11. Judith Butler, "The Sensibility of Critique: A Response to Asad and Mahmood," in *Is Critique Secular? Blasphemy, Injury, and Free Speech* (Berkeley, Calif: Townsend Center for the Humanities, 2009), 115; henceforth cited in the text by page number.

political matters. Indeed, this might be a way to elucidate the
rather conventional notion that, especially in the democratic
polis, reflexivity and interrogation directed toward all established
truths was an expected political responsibility. Because the one
who differentiates is also the one who differs, the interrogation
cannot be limited to the objective realm alone; it is, at once,
also self-interrogation, which is why critique falters if it is not
simultaneously self-critique (this is elementary dialectics). The
bottom line is that the authorization of critique cannot be
assumed to exist in any a priori position but must be intermi-
nably submitted to (self-)critique.

There is an elementary stipulation here that must nonetheless be underlined. The requisite dimension of self-critique in
every critical decision does not mean some sort of circular or
tautological self-referentiality—the self-referential paradox of
logicians—except in an absolutely literal sense (simply the critical reference to "self"), which is, as such, terribly limiting and
rather meaningless beyond its literalism. Structurally speaking,
there is in fact a figure of doubling back onto the source from
which a decision emanates or the ground from which a decision is enacted, which we call "self." But by virtue of this doubling back, the position or figure called "self" is consequently
displaced, or perhaps even internally fissured, differentiated.
(Per its original signification, I repeat, *krisis* enacts a differentiation both on the field of inquiry/judgment and on the one
who performs inquiry/judgment.) Therefore, the "self" in self-
critique is a kind of precarious position, not a position that is
wholly bounded, stable, and given. Surely, this can never signify the collapse between a definitive subject and a definitive
object of judgment or decision (*krisis*). In a simple way, when
a subject becomes its own object (of critical knowledge), it is
dispossessed of its presumed sovereignty, even if for a moment.
But even a moment can never be recuperated intact. Because
decisions are always enacted in time—all critique inhabits and
mobilizes a specific temporality; all critique is always historical
and worldly because it is made by real men and women in the

course of their living in a specific world (their "proper" world and the world "as such")—no subject position (self) is locked in place as the *archē* of decision. If, as a result of (self-)critique, the subject position may be said (or perceived) to be sovereign (yet again), this sovereignty is other to the one before the moment of critique. Autonomy is predicated on the enactment of self-alteration.[12]

Asad attempts a somewhat similar genealogy of the Greek term, correctly accentuating the fact that the presumption of critique to any sort of universal reason is entirely the doing of European modernity. He also adds to the mix what I agree is a crucial affinity of *krisis* with *parrhēsia*, which he indexes through Michel Foucault's rendering of it as fearless speech. An additional way, however, to understand *parrhēsia*, more literally and precisely, is by way of the French expression that Jacques Derrida insists on, particularly in his discussion of the institution of literature: *tout dire*.[13] This means not only to say everything (that is, to speak frankly) but also to say anything, including that which may not yet be, strictly speaking, sayable, including what is presently unsayable, perhaps as yet inconceivable or even impossible. Asad, however, leaving behind even Foucault's historical framework of the ancient genealogy (which is already slanted by a preference for the Stoics), devalues the notion of *parrhēsia* by linking it first to Christian confessional practices, as they arise in the Middle Ages, and subsequently to Kantian critique and its mode of rationalist-

12. I develop this idea further and in relation to the epistemology of sexual difference in "On Self-Alteration," *Parrhesia* 9 (Spring 2010): 1–17, http://www.parrhesiajournal.org/.

13. See, indicatively, Jacques Derrida, "'This Strange Institution Called Literature': An Interview with Jacques Derrida," in *Acts of Literature*, ed. Derek Attridge (New York: Routledge, 1992), 33–75, and "The University without Condition," in *Without Alibi*, ed. Peggy Kamuf (Stanford, Calif.: Stanford University Press, 2002), 202–37. See also Michel Foucault, *Fearless Speech* (New York: Semiotext(e), 2001).

transcendentalist ethics. This is because Asad reads backward into *parrhēsia* a Christian-derived notion of service to truth. No doubt, both in Christianity and in Kantianism, though obviously in different terms, the critical faculty is authorized by a priori structures of truth, whereby the frankness of speech is measured by how faithful the speaker/critic is to truth's dictum. However, what sort of *parrhēsia* is it—indeed, even more, what sort of critique is it—when the ultimate authorizing principle, the *archē* of truth, is not itself subjected to fearless, guiltless, radical interrogation? This is a question that Asad never poses.

If either *parrhēsia* or critique must be necessarily hinged on the regime of truth—this would not be my preferred way to go, but for the sake of argument—it could work only if critique distinguished itself as the great demon that haunts the regime of truth. In other words, it could never be reduced to what Asad identifies as the core principle of Christian and meta-Christian ethics: "the will to be obedient to truth." If it is going to be worthy of its name and its project, critique cannot be obedient to anything. It would have to exist outside the command-obedience structure; it would have to be, in this precise sense, *an-archic.*

One could easily protest that in my argument critique creates its own command structure, which then forces every critical decision into some sort of obedience. But if this is deemed to be a command structure at all, it is unlike any command structure we recognize as worthy of the name because no command framework presides over this structure and no command is issued from the outside. Critique issues its own commands and then follows them—not obeys them (the difference is huge)— always by questioning them. In other words, a decision is made to follow this (self-) command by means and as a result of raising a question (critique) about it. A decision can be made just as well not to follow this command, and then this command lapses. In this sense, the command structure I am presenting is provisional; it cannot be set up as a command-obedience structure by rules issued and implemented outside it. It precipitates a decision that has no foundation in anything that exists prior or exterior to it, for it is an instance of creation, of social-historical action in the course of time that it alters as a result, even if this alteration of the course of time cannot be measured and may not even be visible. In this respect, it is also a recognition of the ultimate groundlessness of human existence, on which societal institutions, laws, traditions, governing structures, and the like are built without ever abolishing it, even if they presume or proclaim to do so.

I understand what sorts of unsettling questions may be raised by this sort of framework. One can easily say: "What kinds of standards are being employed here? Anything goes. On what basis can you tell what is moral and what is not, what is good or bad, and so on?" The question of the grounds of distinction, of differentiation of the field, is crucial. But if critique is to be rigorous with regard to its requisite self-interrogation, no grounds of distinction or differentiation can be established a priori or once and for all. One must always engage in deciding these terms. And this raises the political stakes and the stakes of responsibility. It is in this very sense—and not in the Kantian sense, which always has the safeguard of Reason—that critique is the conditional regime of freedom, if we want to use this term seriously and not in a condition of submission or obedience, if we want this term to mean engaging the reality of what is without feeling compelled by what is said about what is.[14]

From the standpoint he cultivates here, Asad would find such a notion of freedom in critique preposterous. Even the basic skepticism in critique, which is arguably intrinsic to its most archaic signification, is reduced by Asad to an (at best) ethical-rational but ultimately scientific exegetical apparatus that seeks

---

14. Much can be learned here from Luc Boltanski's Adorno Lectures, published as *On Critique: A Sociology of Emancipation* (Cambridge: Polity Press, 2011).

to exhaust the meaning of any object, to rationally extinguish all mystery. Not surprisingly, for Asad the overall schema is akin to how the textual hermeneutics of Protestantism produce a secularizing apparatus that evolves into the humanist scientism and technologism of today. In both registers, Asad discerns a whole machinery of critique that operates according to "the insistent demand that reasons be given for everything." This then serves to prove that "every critical discourse has institutional conditions that define what it is, what it recognizes, what it aims at, what it is destroying—and why" (55).[15]

No dispute can be made about the last statement—there is nothing neutral in critique, as I have already insisted, and, of course, no critique exists outside a specific worldly encounter. But what Asad has in mind is essentially the model of a scientific laboratory, where the idea of "reasons being given for everything" is dictated by none other than the regime of calculation: it can refer only to the demand for either aetiology or causality—that is, strictly speaking, the monological arithmetic of *archē* as singular principle and singular origin. What is silenced here is the constitutive demand of the ancient notion of *krisis*: Aristotle's *logon didonai*, of which "reasons given" would be a linguistically correct but rather impoverished interpretation. Instead, the precise translation of *logon didonai* is accountability: the demand to make explicit one's terms of decision and be held accountable for both having acted on their

15. This is what gives credence to Butler's rejoinder to Asad that he underestimates or misjudges his Foucault. Foucault would never forget that all discourses take place within institutional conditions, but this does not keep him from arguing in favor of critique as an ethos, a specific attitude that bears in mind precisely this frame of institutional conditions that both the action (or the subject) of critique and the object of critique inhabit while enacting critique nonetheless. Butler does not put it this way, but she shows exactly how Foucault subjects Kant and his notion of critique to critique without following the Kantian dictum that even critique must be submitted to critique by the *technē* of Reason. Asad is still arguing against Kant. See Butler, "Sensibility of Critique," 108–20.

basis and having disclosed them. For a critic who fully under-
stands that critical work is never neutral and always takes place
in a field of contention, this may often be a polemical task. It
is always a political task. This is precisely why the conditions of
practicing secular criticism, however institutional one wants to
interpret them to be, are never reducible to professional knowledge. Let us not forget how vehemently Edward Said assailed
discourses of expertise as discourses of obedience to mastery.
Secular criticism is a practice that defies mastery. Secular criticism is indeed skeptical to the core, and to see this as a form of
"secular heroism" is utterly puzzling.

I am referring to Asad's conclusion of this meditation, a
single sentence set apart from the rest of the text: "The 'critical
attitude' is the essence of secular heroism" (55). He leaves this
peculiar wording unelucidated. A careful reader would discern
an echo from a passing reference early in his text to Kant's
defense of the Enlightenment: "To engage in critique, as the
West has done for several centuries, is equivalent to living in Enlightenment: living heroically, as Kant put it in the beginning
of that venture" (47). I suspect that here Asad is referring to
Kant indexing the Horatian exhortation "*Sapere Aude!*" (Dare
to know!) as the quintessential motto for the Enlightenment.
Permit me, first of all, to doubt whether "heroic" is the proper
characterization of this call to dare, but in any case it is Asad's
use of the word that matters, not whether it is accurately reflec-
tive of Kant's thinking, especially given the concluding motto
"The 'critical attitude' is the essence of secular heroism"—in
which the qualification "secular" is in fact the crucial term in
contention.

I suspect, given Asad's discursive demeanor in this essay, that
the heroic is proposed here with a certain irony. In a "Western"
discursive trajectory, the heroic carries primarily pagan associa-
tions, traditionally, in this respect, contrasted with the pious,
which would primarily signify things "Christian." My suspicion
is bolstered by Asad's extensive discussion not only of how the
rational-critical tradition emerges from the Christian practices

of pious pursuit of truth but also, more specifically, of how the notorious lecture of Pope Benedict XVI at Regensburg (2006) drew a direct connection between a Hellenic tradition of critique and its Christian elaboration, lamenting in fact what he called "the dehellenization of Christianity." I have written about the pope's argument extensively—quite differently (and more critically) than Asad —but we would stray off course for me to rehearse this here.[16] What is revealing for my specific purposes is how Asad uses this incident to issue a backhanded dismissal of a pagan cosmology, which he duly calls "heroic," as a possible source of resignification of the secular in the modern world. Moreover, what conventionally belies dismissive references to "heroism" is an aversion to any sort of tragic sensibility, even though in fact, as far as I am concerned, the domain of the tragic can never be relegated simply to the heroic. So the backhanded dismissal of the heroic is indicative of an unwillingness to confront the perplexing question of the tragic, a question that trips up all easy narratives of both secularization and critique of secularization that implicate Judeo-Christianity with secularism in the modern "Western" world.

In a cognitive universe adulterated by Christian (and Christianized) ethics, the tragic is at best incomprehensible and most often abhorrent, even after Nietzsche's unforgettable lesson. The attachment to the heroic as a designation of the tragic is meant precisely to mask this abhorrence. For what is tragic, in the last instance, is the condition of existence in a worldly universe that lacks all guarantees. Less maligned, but equally misunderstood, is the skeptical, which is either turned easily into the cynical or neutralized by association with some sort of Cartesian faculty spiraling into endless rationalist second-guessing. But my sense of the critical and the secular demands that we exceed both the imperious court of Reason and the

---

16. See "The Present of a Delusion" in *Paul and the Philosophers*, ed. Hent de Vries and Ward Blanton (New York: Fordham University Press, 2013).

humble comfort of Piety—therefore, in both cases, the command to obey the regime of Truth. The critical and the secular
have more to do with the skeptical and the tragic, as I just
sketched them, where the demand to make a decision can never
be abrogated or outmaneuvered. To repeat, the terrain of the
skeptical and the tragic is crossed simultaneously by both interrogation and imagination—indeed, the "exercise of an unrealistic imagination," in Jane Bennett's memorable phrase, which
is a whole other way of rendering Kant's call to dare: not merely
dare to know but dare to imagine, dare to know by imagining
what may not be presently knowable.[17] This is the crossroads of
poiein, the political infinitive of altering what exists by thinking
otherwise.

Poiētic thinking does not seek to absolve the world of its uncertainty, does not seek the incontestable, but submits its knowledge to the precariousness of living beings making history.
Verifiability, in poetic thinking, cannot be an outside process,
authorized by some other modality or standard. The process of
establishing truth is the very process of making truth (in the full
sense of *poiein*), a process that is tantamount to the making (and,
of course, always the unmaking) of history. "To submit truth to
history" is another way of saying "to submit truth to critique," as
explained earlier. And the skeptical element of critique, so long
as it does not undo itself by serving as an alibi for imposing certainty (Cartesian doubt followed by truth-finding analysis), is
indeed an essential element of *poiētic* (trans)forming.

It may thus be apparent why to the posed question "Is critique secular?" I responded yes unequivocally, without hedging
in some terrain of so-called neutrality. One makes a decision,
yes or no, in order precisely to raise the stakes of the question.
Anything else, I fear, compromises the interrogative potential
of the secular from the outset. My response leaves no room for

---

17. See Jane Bennett, *Vibrant Matter: A Political Ecology of Things* (Dur-
ham, N.C.: Duke University Press, 2010), 15.

the secular to cruise on its own epistemological assumptions. Insofar as critique can never be anything less than self-critique, the certainty of weighing the secular with the critical is precisely to plunge the domain of the secular into the uncertainty of its own interrogation. Whether we like it or not, this is the domain of the dialectic of Enlightenment, which has nothing to do with either neutrality or the imperiousness of Reason.

The whole point of speaking of *poiein* in relation to secular criticism is to drive a wedge against the standard position that critique is rationalist and objectivist, that it is about neutral judgments of things as they are. I advocate instead a critique that, rather than judging things as they are, alters things, changes what they are. In fact, to be accurate, I would argue that judging things to be as they are actually alters things. This can certainly be debated, but not as a formal proposition. In this argument the *poiētic* becomes a crucial element in decisions of judgment (critique) because every critical decision, at some level (however remote), is involved in the shaping of form and therefore the changing of form, including, as I said, changing one's own form. And the *poiētic* cannot be reduced to the rational, the analytical. It's not that it doesn't involve the rational and the analytic (or, for that matter, the spiritual), but it certainly exceeds them because it deals with imagining things, with things that may be presently impossible. I expressly link the critical with the *poiētic* because I want to add to the purview of critique something creative, which, I repeat, can also be destructive. For this reason too, I dispute the claims made by Asad and others that critique is sold as a sort of hypergood; in fact, the peril of my argument is that I privilege neither something good nor something bad, and yet I disallow the option of the valueless.

———

Let me conclude by sharing a chance instance of rethinking that is pertinent to this discussion. Recently I was asked to elucidate a phrase from Aristotle's *Poetics*—a notorious phrase that has caused much consternation: "With respect to the requirements of art, a probable impossibility is always preferable to an improbable possibility" [*Pros te gar tēn poiēsin airetōteron pithanon adynaton ē apithanon kai dynaton; Poetics* xxv.17].[18] I confess that in light of writing this essay, this mysterious phrase uncannily resonated like never before. Improbable possibility (*apithanon kai dynaton*) pertains to things that are unlikely to happen, even though they are in the realm of possibility or visibility. They may be rare things, but they are indeed mundane things; they belong to an already-existing world to which, were they to occur, they would be merely an extension. But the object of reflection in this text is tragic poetics, theater, a kind of *poiein* that must seek to (re)fashion things mythical, things meaningful to this world but constituted of an order that challenges the limits of this world, things that may indeed appear to be impossible in the present time—at this moment in history in which the drama is conducted—but cannot be said to be generically impossible, impossible for all time.

The qualifier of the phrase is "with respect to the requirements of art [*poiēsis*]". For art to be poetic, it must engage in creating/shaping/transforming aspects of reality. Hence, for art, the impossible is fair game. However, because art also needs to be valued and evaluated according to certain standards of excellence (this is precisely the agonistic nature of theater in the *polis*), the impossible needs to be qualified as well. Hence the likely impossible is preferable to what might be unlikely impossible. The likely impossible might be said to stretch the meaning of *adynaton*; it pertains to an impossibility that will ultimately

18. The phrase also occurs earlier in the following variation: "Accordingly, [the poet] should prefer probable impossibilities to improbable possibilities" [*proaireisthai te dei adynata eikota mallon ē dynata apithana; Poetics* xxiv.10]. Using *eikota* instead of *pithana* is not curious and gives us further insight into this otherwise inscrutable phrase. Although the two words are within the same range of signification, *eikota* can also be rendered as *euloga*—things that are well within reason, even if impossible, things that, were they to become possible, would belong to our language, to our horizon of visibility, our phantasmatic inventory.

alter the range of *dynamis* (capacity, power). The great poets/ tragedians are distinguished precisely in that they can bring the impossible within their dynamic range, their *poiētic* power.

Of course, for Aristotle, the impossible in art could never have the same status as the impossible in reality. We moderns say without much hesitation that there is nothing impossible in art. But this way we tend to forget that art (like everything else) is not value free. Not all impossibles or impossibilities are the same. It is those impossibilities that somehow enable us to shape reality more profoundly—those impossibilities that matter to reality, that are critical to reality, that bring reality to judgment, to *krisis*—that give art (*poiēsis*) its existentially altering, its political, meaning.

TWO

Detranscendentalizing the Secular

My interest here is twofold: First, I want to reiterate in practice how the metaphysics of secularism can be subjected to secular criticism. This will serve to clarify further why I consider critiques of secularism that privilege religious morality, whether as modes of knowledge or of political action, to be no more than alternative metaphysical propositions without justification other than being merely alternative. Second, by extension, I want to underline a critique of heteronomous politics as the bottom line of secular criticism, regardless of whether this politics conceives itself as secular or religious; hence the interrogation of privileging transcendence as an emancipatory trope in a variety of discourses. To this end, let me just put on the table certain assertions, not as axiomatic grounds but as mere anchorings or points of departure for a broader inquiry.

In the simplest sense, I understand the secular as a nonsubstantive, conditional, and differential domain of human action; therefore—speaking precisely—a worldly one. By contradistinction, I identify secularism as an institutional term that represents a range of projects in the exercise of power (particularly in relation to state mechanisms) that often tends toward certain a priori and dogmatic substantiations outside the specific historical field, which is why it may be called secularist metaphysics. If it is not positioned in relation to the historical terms (secularization, secularism) that shadow it with specific signification, the use of the term "secular" as a substantive, like all such adjectival perversions by the rules of the English language, is open to misleading essentialism. Although I advocate the emancipatory potentialities of the secular—indeed, with the aspiration of reconceptualizing and enriching the emancipatory domain of the secular—I explicitly target the metaphysics of secularism, in fact from within the domain and as the work of the secular, as an act of secular criticism. This is why it is crucial that the metaphysics of secularism not be equated with theological metaphysics and that secularism not be considered another sort of religion; this second claim is one of the most politically reactionary positions of antisecularist thinking.

Let us consider more specifically the two historical terms that shadow the secular, which also should be distinguished from each other. First, secularization is a historical process. It names the activity of working on and thus transforming an object—in this case, a prevalent theological social imaginary. As a process, it must be understood to be unfinished by definition. Those who claim secularization's finality are as misguided as those who claim that secularization (in the West) is nothing but a continuation of Christianity by other means. Even Carl Schmitt's celebrated phrase in *Political Theology* ("All significant concepts of the modern theory of the state are secularized theological concepts") fails because of its incapacity to account for the work of the participle "secularized." For something to be secularized cannot possibly mean that it remains as it was before. Whatever the theological traces in modern societies and state structures, a transformation of the meaning of the theological, at the very least, has taken place. Transformation does not mean annihilation of the object, nor does it mean mere

dissimulation or renaming of the object. In fact, precisely because the transformation of the object alters the terms of relation to it, secularization is a process whose theological object,
in some partial way, evades it, thereby ever renewing its pursuit. Thus, whatever its ideologically proclaimed teleology by
secularists of all kinds, secularization remains unfinished, perhaps even unfinishable. This is its greatest power.

Secularism, to the contrary, is an institutional term that
pertains less to a process than a reproduction of a set of definitions, indeed, even a set of commands, that encounter history
as a project of power. The distinction is crucial. Although secularization could be understood as a process that seeks to detranscendentalize the social imaginary (if I may put it this way),
secularism has always been, historically speaking, vulnerable to
a retranscendentalizing process. One can thus speak of secularism's own metaphysics in the sense that as a set of principles
that posit themselves independently of historical reality, secularism operates according to its own transcendental commands.
Even here, however, to equate secularism's metaphysics with
Christianity's metaphysics would be a crucial error whose grav-
est danger (among many) would be to consider the West a
continuous and unalterable entity, the very thing that avid
Eurocentrists claim. Incidentally, I should add the obvious:
Insofar as secularism becomes dogma, it assumes that secularization has ended.

In relation to these two historical shadows, the "secular" is
a term whose conceptual terrain is conditional in the sense
that it finds various historical expressions, each of which needs
to be evaluated on its own terms even if the impetus is to gen-
eralize. The secular is not given once and for all and thus cannot be totalized and bounded; it has a differential history. In
this respect, it is a precarious term as a substantive because
it is nonsubstantial. (For this same reason, I avoid the term
"secularity," which denotes a substantial condition, even if it is
historically determined, which neutralizes its conditionality.)
It is by reconsidering the secular as conditional, as (self-)criti-

cal—which is key to making a demand to detranscendentalize the secular—that we can do the double work of criticizing the metaphysics of secularism and antisecularism at the same time.

I agree that a critique of secularism should begin with de-Christianizing or perhaps even de-Westernizing its content, but to assume an antisecularist position in the process of this critique would ultimately uphold this content as the demon opposite. I certainly concur with Wendy Brown's assessment of "secularism as an instrument of empire"; nonetheless, my interest is counterposed to her stated one.[1] The challenge for me is to understand how the secular can work against empire and even against the history of secularism's complicity with nationalist, colonialist, and imperialist practices.[2] For this reason, the many politics of antisecularism, whatever standpoint they may come from, need to be deconstructed specifically at their points of convergence. I cannot but underline Simon During's indisputable observation that "the structural link between European conservative political theology and post-colonial anti-secularism makes for strange encounters."[3] Saba Mahmood's claim for the "normative impetus *internal* to secularism" (my emphasis) and Talal Asad's approving reiteration of it exemplify this peculiar encounter.[4]

1. See Wendy Brown, "Idealism, Materialism, Secularism?, http://www.ssrc.org/blogs/immanent_frame/2007/10/22/idealism-materialism-secularism/.

2. This was the impetus of a pioneering special issue of the journal *boundary 2*, "Critical Secularism," edited by Aamir Mufti: *boundary 2* 31, no. 2 (Summer 2004).

3. See Simon During, "The Mundane against the Secular," http://www.ssrc.org/blogs/immanent_frame/2007/11/10/the-mundane-against-the-secular/.

4. I refer initially to Saba Mahmood's "Secularism, Hermeneutics, and Empire: The Politics of Islamic Reformation," *Public Culture* 18, no. 2 (2006): 323–47, and Talal Asad's "Secularism, Hegemony, and Fullness," http://www.ssrc.org/blogs/immanent_frame/2007/11/17/secularism-hegemony-and-fullness/, and subsequently to their contributions to the volume *Is Critique Secular?*

If secularization indeed at some point takes a normative track (whereby the law of God becomes automatically reconfigured as Law as such—Law as God, one might say), and secularism therefore emerges as a new metaphysics, my response is surely not to embrace an allegedly liberational space of "native-religious" sentiment suppressed by colonial or imperial power, but rather to unpeel the layers of normativity from secularist assumptions and reconceptualize the domain of the secular. At the very least, the alleged normative impetus of secularism ought to be contested no less than the normative impetus of x or y religion or science. In all cases, it is absurd to speak of the internal axiomatically. Instead, what is *internalized* under specific political conditions should be the target of such interrogation.

Most recently fashionable antisecularist positions stand at the forefront of an alarming conservative trend that takes the critical edge out of postcolonial thinking by turning it, even if cryptically, into cultural identity politics. One wonders why the critique against Western domination has to be antisecularist. Why it *has to be*. From a basic standpoint, it is the easiest gesture, a kind of facile no-brainer, but in this haste it commits two consubstantial errors: (1) it equates the West and all its excesses with the excess of secularism; and (2) it forgets that much of what establishes the West (its domination and its excesses) is and continues to be antisecular. The latter problem is arguably outmaneuvered by Gil Anidjar's equation of secularism with Christianity, but to the extent that this remains an equation, a tautological collapse that disavows the transformative process of secularization, it merely reverts to the first category.[5] Even if we assume that at the very least, secularization registers a mutation of the Christian imaginary, our

<hr />

Blasphemy, Injury, and Free Speech (Berkeley, Calif.: Townsend Center for the Humanities, 2009). I address parts of these arguments later.

5. See Gil Anidjar, "Secularism," in *Semites: Race, Religion, Literature* (Stanford, Calif.: Stanford University Press, 2008), 39–66.

attention yields most if it is focused on the transformative elements that signify a mutation. Even if we were to underline theological remnants in secular metaphysics ("In God we trust" etc.), our attention yields most if it is focused on them as remnants of meaning in a new configuration of meaning. Even if we imagine the relation between Christianity and secularism under Hegelian conditions of *Aufhebung*, whereby the sublated element is somehow preserved, what really challenges our attention is indeed the meaning of preservation in the larger signifying context that includes abolition, augmentation, dissolution, suspension, and so forth—the full significational range of *Aufhebung*. The disregard of discontinuity in secularization not only reproduces the hegemonic image of the "continuous West" but also occludes the complication of the politics of modernity, the very core of the dialectic of Enlightenment argument.

The problem with naïve antisecularist anti-Westernism is not so much categorizing the enemy; no more or less than "Islam," the "West" is a useless categorization and false in anything but rhetorical fashion. The problem lies in presuming that the secular is the hidden core identity of the enemy. Postcolonial repudiations of the secular—at least those waged from the convenient position of the "secular West"—should at least consider the political consequences of their de facto alliance with right-wing American Christianity and fellow warmongers of empire, whose avowed enemies, next to the evils of Islam, are the secular humanists who threaten American integrity.[6]

6. I recall explicitly Mitt Romney's "Faith in America" speech given at the George Bush Presidential Library on December 6, 2007, several years before his alliance with the Christian Right in order to mount an attack on the Obama presidency. In the same year, Newt Gingrich railed against "the growing culture of radical secularism" in a eulogy of Jerry Falwell (see the *Washington Post*, May 20, 2007, A04). I am sure that I could put together a list of references that would go on for several pages per year. And yet, antisecularists in the academy would remain unperturbed.

Moreover, we have to be equally careful about ascribing to secularism a religious quality in a straightforward sense (this is what Mitt Romney or Newt Gingrich do explicitly, but it is also the outcome of many of secularism's critics). To obliterate the difference between the religious and the secular is to deal oneself a hand in which the cards are all the same despite their different colors or values. It is one thing to speak of the metaphysics of secularism and another to equate secularism with religion. (Indeed, the task is even to liberate the secular conceptually from its determinant opposition by the religious.) The embattled terrain emerges precisely because of this difference, and the most interesting question this terrain produces is : can a secular worldview overcome its metaphysical (or transcendentalist) propensity? Or even more, can we imagine a nontheomorphic world? And what sort of social imaginary would give meaning to this process? These questions, which might be said to frame the disjunction between the Christian and the secular, must be grounded in the fact of the "failure" of secularization, as the incompleteness of secularization is often falsely named.

In the same vein I would add the historical exigency of differentiating the worldliness of Christianity since the Early Modern era from secular worldliness, if the secular (as I consider it) consists in recognizing the ubiquity of finitude as a basic operating principle, thereby placing the possibility of transcendence continually in question. Such worldliness would be configured in terms of the body and all its murky relations to unstable matter and would therefore be differentiated from the supposed worldliness of rationalist metaphysics or of the transcendental Ego. It is there that we might locate the ground of secularism's metaphysics, and it is there—in this metaphysics—that secularism's complicity in the history of colonialist and imperialist domination may be found. Whatever worldliness is supposedly signified by the transcendental rationality of Descartes, for example, is by my account measured in terms of its historical affinity with Christian theological forms. Cartesian autonomy exists via a theological *epistemē*, specifically the monotheistic identity principle. Formally speaking, at least, the epistemological underpinning of "I think, therefore I am" is found in the absolute identitarian monism of "I am that I am"; the symbolic universe continues to rest on the model of authority being determined according to the tautological self-possession of the divine. The fact that Descartes can prove by mathematical logic the existence of God or the immortality of the soul does not make him a materialist thinker. Indeed, the mathematical prowess of the Cartesian imaginary serves as the epitome of heteronomous veiling because it authorizes and legitimates with the power of reason humanity's willful submission to oblivion regarding its capacity to make God exist.

The discrepancy between the material and the nonmaterial is precisely where the problem of transcendence needs to be posed. An act of despiritualization—should we choose to limit the secular in this way (I'm taking the crudest secularist line, to which I obviously don't subscribe)—does not obliterate the nonmaterial; it simply puts it in an antagonistic situation whereby its signification becomes mutable according to whatever social-historical forces are at play. In simple terms, it deprives the nonmaterial of a priori determination; it politicizes the nonmaterial—which does not mean producing a politics out of some transcendental vision but, to the contrary, submitting the transcendental vision to political interrogation and critique. The transcendental a priori (whether Cartesian or Kantian) bars even considering that meaning is mutable and that signification is consistently enigmatic beneath whatever determinations. And as far as it pertains to an Ego construction (the rational mind, the ethical subject, etc.), even to articulate transcendence in language—even if in the very wish for transcendence, in the seductive fantasy of its possibility—means to have already suspended one's own enigmatic condition, the aporia of oneself inhabiting the enigma of living worldly being. In the sense that the enigmatic is what refuses to be closed (to be self-enclosed) strictly speaking, the actual articulation of transcendence—in any theoretical system, theological or rationalist—is impossible except as its own demise.

Yet, transcendence is professed all over the place, often gratuitously and with the certainty that it is somehow intrinsically understood, all the while successfully laboring, as Adorno would put it, to keep secretive the signifying mode, the language, that possesses it—that possesses us.[7] Even the so-called secular end of religion by virtue of Christianity does not consist, as Marcel Gauchet claims (and Charles Taylor concurs, though with a different aim), in the abolition of transcendence by a production of immanence. Instead, it signifies the *internalization* of transcendence, which deactivates in turn the immanent creativity of changing oneself into another (self-alteration), which is essential to confronting one's own enigma as an autonomous person. This internalization is precisely at work in Kantian rationalist morality, considered by many the epitome of secularist morality. The provenance of Kantian morality is due not to shifting a Christian moral command-obedience model from the agency of God to the agency of the subject, but the reverse: putting the subject in God's place, creating a transcendental moral subject against which all human praxis is measured. The metaphysics of Kant's rationalism is thus a problem not as cause but as symptom. Reason becomes theological, not because reason is inherently or residually theological, but because the architectural frame of morality in Western modernity remains religious (Christian). The epistemological difference between these two modes of explanation is cataclysmic.

———

The point of this difference is precisely what Charles Taylor's monumental work on the subject misses at the core. As a story,

7. Theodor W. Adorno, "On Lyric Poetry and Society," in *Notes on Literature*, vol. 1 (New York: Columbia University Press, 1990), 37–54.

A Secular Age rivals Hans Blumenberg's *The Legitimacy of the Modern Age* (which, curiously, it ignores) and may be said to belong to the largely neglected genre of speculative history. It is a work of a lifetime's worth of erudition—about this there can be no argument—but the easiest thing one can do is to praise it. The best and most profound insight this work has to offer is precisely that the domains of thought and history it privileges must be interrogated in order to stand as departure points for further thinking. This interrogation and evaluation cannot stay simply at the level of the story but must extend to what authorizes the story: Taylor's (conscious or unconscious, explicit or implicit) politics. I will address this politics by limiting myself here to an examination of Taylor's understanding of immanence and humanism, keeping within the parameters of the broader task of detranscendentalizing the secular.

In Taylor's hands, these two notions present an intertwined set of problems. Already as a naming, Taylor's "exclusive humanism" is a polemical notion and hardly accurate in regard to humanism's multiple and multivalent historical realities. When all is said and done, exclusive humanism turns out to be an all-inclusive notion for Taylor; little else that passes for humanism is deemed nonexclusive. Taylor mentions "various forms of deep ecology" in the contemporary world as the only possibility that may elude this exclusivity, while he dismisses the import of any ancient "nonexclusive" worldviews, which as moderns we would identify as humanist: Epicureanism, for example.[8] Italian Renaissance humanism is exempted, I presume,

8. In the preface, Taylor speaks of "the unbridgeable gulf between Christianity and Greek philosophy" (Charles Taylor, *A Secular Age* [Cambridge, Mass.: Harvard University Press, 2007], 17; henceforth cited in the text). Strictly speaking, I would agree with the statement, but not at all in the baffling terms in which it is made, where Taylor takes as a distillation of Greek philosophy Socrates's explicit invocation of a preferable afterlife (in Plato's *Crito*), which he then opposes to Christ's self-conscious embrace of life in the acceptance of death—hence the alleged gulf. Not only is this Platonic desire,

because it is still based on a Christian viewpoint—although this itself, as an overall assessment, can be doubted—while no mention is made of Islamic humanism in medieval Baghdad and al-Andalus, which, as George Makdisi has shown, is as materialist and worldly (in terms of its historical performance) as anything.[9] Moreover, a whole strain of thought that is traced to Nietzsche (although it indeed might go back to Spinoza) and includes what is generally named post-structuralism is deemed plainly antihumanist and is thus ipso facto excluded from the purview of exclusive humanism. This assessment is hasty, to say the least, and my hunch is that excluding this strain of thought by naming it "antihumanism" merely serves to render the notion of exclusive humanism tighter and uncomplicated.

In any case, the mark of exclusion here concerns the transcendental—in fact, the transcendental signified by/as the religious. Kantian thought, for example, is deemed to belong to the trajectory of exclusive humanism even though transcendentalism is essential to it. The exclusionary and the immanent are entwined in Taylor's mind as qualifications of each other. The "buffered self" is an exclusionary self, and the "immanent frame" is, in the last instance, a frame of closure, of self-enclosure, whose greatest failure is that it inhibits humanity's openness to

---

in the persona of Socrates, counter to several centuries of Greek ways of life (from the earliest indications in the Homeric epics onward) and thereby a perverse metonymy for Greek philosophy as such, but also the invocation of Christ embracing life in the world by accepting death flies in the face of the most basic of the Pauline precepts on which the Christian Church (especially in its Latin derivation) is founded. It is the Resurrection, the conquest of death (not the Crucifixion, the fact of death) that is quintessential to Pauline Christianity. But such misconstructions are all over this text, as are the invectives against Nietzsche as being a death-driven philosopher who facilitates fascist thinking. Indeed, Taylor's panic before the obstacle of Nietzsche deserves a separate philosophical analysis.

9. See George Makdisi, *The Rise of Humanism in Classical Islam and the Christian West* (Edinburgh: Edinburgh University Press, 1990).

the transcendental. Exclusive humanism, then, is in essence dehumanizing, and Taylor's call is for a rehumanization based on a transcendentalist imaginary that is entirely, in the end, authorized by Christianity.

Yet Taylor refuses to theologize. One might say that he treats the religious element in a way analogous to the way in which Freud conceives the unconscious—as inherited psychic material—thereby circumventing the theological frame altogether. This enables him to reside in the domain of the secular even while his entire work is against it, but to shield in this way the fact that the epistemological framework of his critique resides outside secular authorization. Although it is a simplification, it is accurate to say that Taylor's thought merely extends the tradition of Christian humanism (and hence the totalized discrediting of other forms of humanism), and his underlying impulse is to (re)direct the social imaginary of the secular age against its worldly self-authorization.

There are at least two problems here. The first pertains to the very schema by which Taylor categorizes secularity. Although this schema is not necessarily an incorrect rendition of the historical process, it implicitly assumes that the process of secularization has an end in both senses: purpose and end point. But whatever the purported visions of a social-imaginary orientation toward secular authorization since arguably the twelfth century of Western Christian history, the most substantial significance of secularization is, I repeat, that it is an unfinished project by definition. First, by definition, because it denotes a social imaginary striving for explicit self-authorization, and no self-authorization can come to an end unless it means the end of this self. (It is possible, from an extremely pessimistic but now unfortunately altogether realizable standpoint, that this social imaginary may indeed produce the annihilation of the entire planet, but then none of us will be around to debate the actual causes and reasons of such self-destruction.) Second, unfinished, because—if we bar this suicidal scenario—self-authorization, if it is to be genuine, cannot but remain predicated on self-interrogation and self-alteration. I will return to this second point later on.

The second problem pertains to Taylor's limited configuration of what he calls social imaginary. The fact that he has ignored the monumental work of Cornelius Castoriadis, *The Imaginary Institution of Society* (1965–75), which remains the most accomplished, meticulous, and daring exploration and theorization of this notion, certainly contributes to his limitation. The matter is too vast for discussion here, but let me just say, very simply, that Taylor would never entertain, for example, that "God" is a social-imaginary signification—to speak not just of the Christian God but equally of any other or others—whose history, as social-imaginary signification, is rather precisely accountable and demonstrable. As is, moreover, equally accountable and demonstrable that this very history elucidates the antecedent social imaginary that institutes a specific signification of God (any god or gods): that is, enables it to have meaning, enacts or realizes this meaning in the world, and is thereby socially instituted by it. This aspect, the fact that a social imaginary institutes the society that institutes it in an entirely open-ended dialectical reciprocity, not a sequence of any sort, is especially missing from Taylor's understanding. Missing is also an understanding of the social imaginary as a cracked horizon, if one may put it this way, namely, neither background nor foreground of society's primary significations, which is precisely what enables major epistemic shifts to be created, like the advent of the notion of the One and Only God or the invention of capitalism.

The upshot of this undialectical understanding of social-imaginary institution is not merely the consequently undialectical understanding of modernity or humanism but the very conception (and conceptual privilege) of the notions "buffered self" and "immanent frame." Ultimately, in his heart of hearts (to use a spiritual phrase), Taylor cannot fathom the idea that fullness, total plenitude and fulfillment, can be found in the finite and the fragile, in the ephemeral and the mortal, in the uncertain and the passing. In his heart of hearts, he will doubt this possibility and ultimately dismiss it, dispute its truth, and discard it as a source of transformative (in his language, transcendent) power. Therefore, his understanding of what he calls "spiritual reality" cannot go further than a religious understanding because even when he recognizes the seeking of spiritual reality in "humanist imaginaries," he ends up questioning its true validity. Worse yet, he does not stop reminding us that such modes of ("humanist") life repudiate or denigrate the spiritual, all the while remaining certain that the spirituality of the religious faith he espouses does not in fact ultimately denigrate those modes of life and their own claims to fulfillment.

Most worrisome of all is Taylor's mocking attitude toward what he calls the "therapeutic" (in opposition to the "spiritual"), which at best provides us, he says, with the "dignity of sin" (620). Psychoanalysis bears the worst of the therapeutic register in his argument, with some rather embarrassing mannerisms on his part that circulate the most insipid accusations of psychoanalysis as either a professional justification of the pleasures/ills of the flesh or the mere normalization of people to the routine of bourgeois life. Underneath it all lies Taylor's stipulation that psychoanalysis lacks any sort of moral outcome, which is, of course, true—that is its greatest power. But why should lack of moral outcome mean less profound self-understanding or even inauthentic spirituality? Let us remember that Freud's *Geistigkeit* denotes a collective binding that is as much spiritual as it is intellectual, according to the two parameters of *Geist* but devoid of their Christian trappings—this being precisely the problem for Taylor. Taylor disputes the transformative power of an amoral stance, as if morality is the only redeeming motivation of human spiritual action. Of course, because for him the human spirit is meaningful only as transcendent spirit (whereby the transcendent is determined by an otherworldly

command—but why play with words? a religious command),
no real human spirit, engaged with but unconstrained by an
external moral order, matters at all. In the end, Taylor's portrait of unbelievers as yearning and ultimately unfulfilled is as
impoverished as the portrait of believers as blissed out with
certainty and fulfillment.

Meanwhile, the epistemological parameters of fulfillment
are ultimately left unexamined—or, which is to say the same
thing, resolved by virtue of certain a priori truth standards. What
is "fuller love"? Or rather, in what terms is it to be achieved?
This is not a neutral question, nor is it even simply philosophical (to be determined by its truth-value). It is a political question, and whatever the response, it enacts a specific politics.
Surely, it is a political decision to pit the term "fuller love"
against the term "desire-obsessed mode of spirituality" (631)—a
political decision both in giving these specific names to social
modes, needs, or attributes and in naming which one is more
authentic. There exists here an unannounced but hardly implicit privileging of love over desire (and the metonymic accou-
trements of fullness versus obsession), as if the two can ever
really have an independent meaning. It is an old and conventional trick to designate in the overcoming of *eros* by *agapē* the
shift from the pagan to the Christian imaginary and thereby
deem any modern slippage into the former a brutal regression
toward tragic amorality. I cannot go into detail here, theoreti-
cally, on what subsidizes Taylor's fear of the tragic, but I do want
at least to underline how much this unacknowledged fear is
predicated on the unacknowledged devaluation of *eros*. According to the framework of the "buffered self," *eros* is ultimately
limited (and thus cannot lead to "human flourishing") not
only because the self holds all the reins of signification but because the alterity of another human can never fulfill the demands of the transcendent position. The other is another self,
buffered just as much, and there is thus no possibility of *eros*
producing the transcendent action because it does not engage
(or produce, in effect) a proper alterity. From Taylor's point of

view, the fullness of transcendence is predicated on alterity being external to any self.[10]

I would be the first to agree that "human flourishing" always involves an ecstatic condition, a coming-to-be outside any strictly defined parameters of self, in whatever tradition and social imagination they are to be conceived. The important question, however, is: Where is this outside? Where do we (and how do we) determine this outside to be? The joke about the dissatisfaction with immanence being articulated as in Peggy Lee's famous 1960s song "Is That All There Is?" is quite telling (311). Taylor makes a lot out of the question in the song's title, but as far as the song goes, nothing privileges the question over the answer that completes the refrain: "If that's all there is my friends, then let's keep dancing, let's break out the booze and have a ball." You can certainly choose to treat the answer with contempt, as so much irresponsible, shallow, decadent, or whatever narcissism, but the key here is to ask: What position authorizes you to voice this contempt? At the same time, you can also see the answer as a gesture of fullness—tragic, of course—which is, simultaneously, to ask: From what position is one authorized to claim that the tragic does not in fact bear fullness?

For Taylor—no doubt in sophisticated fashion—an outside must exist as such. This is not necessarily a problem, except that for Taylor this outside must hold primary determining authority. Taylor's whole framework of valuation and determination is heteronomous. As a result, he cannot fathom an alterity that is internal, an immanence that may produce transcendence but is not authorized by transcendence. One of the

10. Interesting in this regard, although it does not engage this presumption against *eros* in Taylor, is a paper by Michael Warner on "Sex and Secularity," delivered on several occasions but not yet published. A glimpse of the argument, but by no means the substance of it, can be found in a post on the Immanent Frame under the title "The Ruse of Secular Humanism," http://blogs.ssrc.org/tif/2008/09/22/the-ruse-of-secular-humanism/.

dire consequences of Taylor's disregard of Castoriadis, insofar as the social imaginary is concerned, is that his understanding of autonomy is still bound by Kantian models. The immanence of autonomy does not mean closure in a purely self-referential or self-sufficient signification, because both the psychic and the political horizons of autonomy, as condition and capacity, are self-alteration. Autonomy is nonsensical as a permanent or complete state, as the property of the thing, which is why it has nothing to do with the imaginary of self-possession or the legacy of possessive individualism that is the crux of liberal law.

Incidentally, it goes without saying, but I guess one always has to repeat it, that autonomy is not about individual units; an autonomous individual can be autonomous only if all other individuals in that shared community or society are autonomous. Autonomy is always social autonomy or is not autonomy at all (just as an individual is always a social individual, not only an individual person within a society but a category of identification that does not and cannot exist outside society). A society that claims that the Law—any mode of law, "secular" or "sacred"—is autonomous is not an autonomous society. "To give oneself the law" means simultaneously "to interrogate the law"—to interrogate both the *archē* and the *telos* of the law, to think of the law otherwise, from the standpoint of dissent. (I am mining here the literal meaning of Rosa Luxemburg's famous notion of *Freiheit der Andersdenkenden*.) In a word, to give oneself the law is to alter the law and to alter oneself in relation to this altering. This is a process that has no beginning or source and, of course, no termination except its final demise. It is also a process that has no foundation. For society to change, the people in that society must change. But for people to change, society must be changed; a different society must emerge. And this difference can be created only by people acting differently within that society and by means of that society; difference cannot be created by extraterrestrials. This is the dynamics of autonomy as self-alteration: an immanent otherness, a way of thinking of oneself otherwise (*Andersdenken*), of enacting oneself as other to oneself. (Hence the requisite theatricality of autonomy, as I understand it, but that is another discussion.) Understanding autonomy as self-alteration dissolves the notion of the "buffered self" and locates the "outside" in the very process or practice of transformation, of the radical capacity to imagine and enact oneself and one's world in a way until now unimaginable.[11]

On the other hand, I understand heteronomy equally simply according to the word itself: being under the law of another. This does not pertain merely to religion, as is often thought—although there cannot be any theistic religion that is not heteronomous, for obvious reasons. Heteronomy pertains as well to any worldly conditions in which the law is, in the last instance, beyond question. Any sense that the law is ultimately unapproachable, inalterable, and, institutionally speaking, greater than the society that has consented to this law it has ultimately created is a heteronomous condition. In fact, heteronomy exists from the very moment a society refuses to acknowledge that it and no one else has created the law of its God, its state, or its universe. In a sense, the most basic term of combating heteronomy is to abolish conditions of metalaw, or beyond the law, or the law as such being a beyond. No one has demonstrated this better than Franz Kafka, whose literature (as theory) trumps any theory of transcendental law, political or theological.[12]

———

My commitment to combating heteronomous politics of whatever form underlies my argument that the critique of religion

11. I develop this point at length in "On Self-Alteration," *Parrhesia* 9 (Spring 2010): 1–17, http://www.parrhesiajournal.org/.

12. Colin Jager misses this very simple point in his criticism of my reading of Taylor. See "Secular Brooding, Literary Brooding," http://blogs.ssrc.org/tif /2008/06/22/secular-brooding-literary-brooding/. I discuss the problem of heteronomy in detail in a separate chapter later in this book.

and the critique of secularism involve similar work—the task of secular criticism. Even when I identify secularism's transcendentalist politics as heteronomous politics—its technological rationalism, the cultural Ego Ideal, the imperialist *mission civilisatrice*, the instrumentalist appropriation of the other, and so on—as, for example, in my exchange with Saba Mahmood, the response is either simple denial or charges of disingenuousness. No doubt, as polarized as the debate has become, such double critiques will be damned from one side if they still hold on to the notion of the secular at all. Mahmood's position, subsequent to her *Politics of Piety* and our exchange, shows a genuine attempt to confront some of these contradictions even if it does not ultimately manage to overcome them. I cannot say the same for Talal Asad, whose positions on the matter of secular criticism are becoming less nuanced over time.

My initial reading of Mahmood's "Secularism, Hermeneutics, and Empire: The Politics of Islamic Reformation" followed four axes of argument. I reiterate them here in order to move on to her subsequent essay on the controversy over the Danish cartoons depicting the Prophet Muhammad:

1. Mahmood predicates her entire argument on an uninterrogated identification of secularism with liberalism. One wonders why her political critique is not addressed to liberalism as such, or why, in her political critique, the ideology of liberalism is reduced to a problem of the secular versus the nonsecular. Let us say that although her target seems to be (by virtue of the argument) the normativity of liberal institutions, her desired enemy is not liberalism but secularism. However, because she does not even raise the question of their equivalence as a preliminary self-critical step in her argument, Mahmood confounds the terrain, possibly hoping that she can hit both targets at once. But this way she misses the fact that you cannot conduct an antisecularist argument simply by attacking liberalism without falling into the habit of argumentation that advances the antiliberal agendas of U.S. Christian Republicanism. This

is one of the ways in which Mahmood's argument is conservative, whether she intends this or not.

Needless to say, I hardly care to defend liberalism. On the contrary, my attempt to reconfigure the domain of the secular against secularism's own statist metaphysics is also a critique of the metaphysics of liberalism as such—both its statist and its market metaphysics. But my intent is not to wage a critique against liberalism per se—not here, anyway—but against heteronomous politics in whatever form it takes, liberal or nonliberal, secularist or religious. The imaginary investment of certain Western (largely Christian) societies in secular institutions—usually (but uncritically) associated with liberal institutions—cannot be the exclusive ground of defining and debating the secular. I understand how convenient this exclusivity is because this way the antisecularist argument draws strength from the condemnation of the U.S. imperialist machinery. But again, this convenience raises the question why a critique of imperialism has to be conducted as a critique of secularism. Why it *has to be*.

2. Mahmood's central thesis is that secularism "proffers remaking certain kinds of religious subjectivities (even if this requires the use of violence)" according to a "normative impetus internal" to it.[13] "Normativity" is indeed her favorite word, and here it flags the U.S. imperialist agenda of forcefully shaping subjectivities in the Islamic world. About this agenda, there can be no argument. But whether this agenda proceeds from a secularist impulse is a matter of debate. I suppose that to the degree that we are talking about practices of the U.S. institutional apparatus, this impulse could be called secularist (among other names). But I don't think that these practices can be so easily considered secular, as Mahmood's own phrasing—"the

---

13. Mahmood, "Secularism, Hermeneutics, and Empire," 328. Hereafter cited in the text by page number.

United States has embarked upon an ambitious theological campaign" (329)—explicitly admits. This conceptual difference is not so fine as to be imperceptible, whether by Mahmood or anybody else. The difference between institutional secularism and the secular as a conditional domain of interrogation is marked by an epistemological chasm.

Then there is the issue of secularism's shaping of subjectivities as such, its "attendant anthropology of the subject" (330). I don't dispute the subjectification that colonialist and imperialist states have enforced on conquered peoples all over the globe (but also—and this is equally important—on their own societies). But there is something naïve in founding one's argument about the ills of the secular imagination solely on the inarguable fact of colonialist/imperialist politics, especially when one dares not even pose the question of what is normative in nonsecular modes of rule. How can one assert that there is no ground for critique of nonsecular modalities of political rule seeking to transform religious (not to mention nonreligious) subjectivities so they conform to a certain politics? Shall we not speak of the "attendant anthropology of the subject" that Mahmood's own ethnographic argument proposes? What agenda authorizes us to remain uncritical of it?

3. Following this logic of confounding liberalism and imperialism with secularism, Mahmood makes a startling association between the imperialist chronicles of the Rand Corporation regarding the inner workings of Islamic societies and certain prominent Muslim reformist thinkers, who are deemed "apostate"—Nasr Hamid Abu Zayd, Hasan Hanafi, and Abdul Karim Soroush—as indicated by such phrasing as "Echoing the Rand report's contention that the Quran is a human rather than a divine text, Abu Zayd argues that the Quran . . . entered history" (337). Do I really need to ask why we need the Rand Corporation to confirm that the Quran is a human rather than a divine text? What is a divine text but what certain humans under certain conditions (which are always historical, even when they are expressed in the most profound

spiritual terms) configure, name, and occasionally worship as divine?

It is one thing for Mahmood to argue that the Quran is divine from the standpoint of a believer. But if she argues that for some people the Quran is divine (as, for others, are the Vedas, the Torah, the Gospels, or the Book of Mormon), she engages in a historical argument about a historical process that institutes a text as divine and—since we are speaking of a social-imaginary institution—continuously reinstitutes a text as divine, as long as is required by a certain society or societies, a certain community or communities, in order to safeguard and reanimate their identity. Missing here is a meditation on what sort of textuality characterizes a sacred text, in which Walter Benjamin's insights would be essential. No politics of the sacred is comprehensible without analysis of the textual authority that animates it, and this is a poetic matter in the deepest sense: the textuality of the sacred pertains to society's *poiein*. I would never discount the vast political power, whether subjugating or insurgent, of a sacred text. But that this power is derived from the text's being regarded as sacred does not mean that it is sacred. Or, that a text derives its political power from being claimed as sacred by a certain society does not mean that it is sacred by divine decree. In other words, the point is not to dispute the sacredness of the text but to raise questions about how this sacredness is authorized.

This is also the case with politics based on transcendental religious commands, all the more specifically when such commands pertain nominally to emancipatory politics. I would never doubt, for instance, the revolutionary inspiration that liberation theology once gave to certain oppressed societies in Central America, the importance of the Christian discourse of salvation in African American narratives of emancipation since the slavery era, or the inarguable power that Islam held for certain insurgent communities in Iraq against American military forces. But as I have said several times, this does not mean that, come postinsurgency time, the time of self-determination, a

politics based on religious command can institute modes of
social autonomy—at least, in known history this has never
happened. There is a foundational reason: A politics based on
a religious command denies the last instance of society's self-
interrogation of who authorizes its self-determination. Not
only does this politics take for granted an external, ahistorical,
heteronomous authorization, namely, divine power; it forbids
the very question. This is not to say, I repeat, that emancipatory
politics cannot emerge from within a religious language. But it
is to say that if it does, it must place this very language in question; it must deauthorize this language as command.

4. Mahmood's dismissal of any argumentative basis for the
Quran as a historical text belies her conviction that neither
Quranic scripture nor Islamic ritual can be treated as a system
of semiotic or symbolic significations. What is operative in
both dismissals is disregard for the literary domain as a proper
epistemological framework, or indeed, disregard of the poetic
as such: "The fact that this understanding of religion and scripture as a system of signs and symbols, ready for a cultured individual to interpret according to her poetic resources, enjoys such
broad appeal is in part what the term *normative secularity* cap-
tures" (343; her italics). How the poetic becomes normative is
one of the most mysterious cognitive steps in Mahmood's entire argument.

Mahmood continues in this vein to reiterate her argument
from *Politics of Piety* that "Muslim women's consensual adop-
tion of the veil" (343) is belittled when it is subjected to analy-
ses that determine it according to its symbolic indications, its
semiotic meaning, its significations of identity, or even its social
instrumentality in regard to sexuality and gender roles. (In this
last sense, one might say that Mahmood's position discredits
arguments that see in the politics of the veil an overt playing
out of sexual difference. I agree—such arguments weaken the
power of sexual difference as both a political and an epistemological category.) Instead, Mahmood argues that the veil claims
"a religious obligation" as "part of a religious doctrine, a divine

edict, or a form of ethical practice, and that it therefore has nothing to do with 'identity' " (343). I understand (and here I also agree with) the terms of her objection to the secularist assessment—whether oppositional (feminist or otherwise) or supportive (as indicative of a woman's right to choose how to identify herself)—that wearing a veil imposes on the gesture an external framework of meaning and thus disregards the gesture's self-determination.

But I am befuddled by her unwillingness to press the critical question in both directions. Is the veil not a sign for the devout Muslim? What is it? An empty signifier? And as a sign, how can it not be activated but in an identity formation? Incidentally, by virtue of the elementary dialectics of institution in any society, no identity formation can ever be conducted entirely within an internal signifying framework; no identity formation can ever be monolithic. One's identity—even under conditions of perfect self-determination (which, of course, never exist in history, but only for the sake of argument)—can never be formed without simultaneously forming the identity of the other against whom (or in difference from whom) one defines oneself.

To argue further: Why is utter and unquestionable obedience to divine/doctrinal edict not an identitary mechanism? This question is never answered by Mahmood because it is not even asked, as if obedience to divine doctrine differs substantially from obedience to nondivine doctrine. (We are talking of strict obedience to doctrine, not negotiation with authority.) If one were to argue seriously that religious obedience is radically different from any other kind of doctrinal obedience, so that it lies beyond the world of symbols, signs, social and communal mechanisms, or principles of identity formation, there are only two options: (1) either the religious experience is totally unworldly and therefore asocial and ahistorical, and in this respect, one can never claim that it bears a politics of piety, or any other politics, for that matter; or (2) the religious experience is utterly irrelevant to any discourse or meditation on society

and can be conducted only in terms of the self-enclosed herme-
neutic universe of mystical thinking, and for this we have,
say, the extraordinary texts of the Kabbalah, of Rumi, or of St.
Teresa de Avila—texts that do not require the authorization of
the sacred to yield their poetic splendor.

In other words, if nonsecular gestures are to bear a certain
politics, they cannot be determined as idiosyncratic or idiomatic gestures; they pertain to an imagined community of some
kind and are therefore implicated in an identity formation of
some kind. It is Mahmood's unwillingness even to entertain the
notion that these gestures are themselves identitary gestures—no
doubt, in their own way, and here the difference between identitary frameworks would be a worthy theoretical pursuit—that
anchors her antisecularist politics to the stealth dogmatism of
nativist identity politics. One yearns here for the intellectual
daring that Frantz Fanon showed in the midst of a real revolutionary situation when he warned us of the pitfalls of national
consciousness, equally unafraid to dismantle colonialist and
postcolonial—and, I might add, "Western" and "non-Western,"
secular and nonsecular—essentialisms alike.

In her subsequent article "Religious Reason and Secular Affect," Mahmood reiterates the line of argument that presumes
a nonsemiotic, nonidentitarian dimension in Muslim devotional practices, this time regarding certain Muslim responses
to the cartoon depictions of the Prophet Muhammad in the
Danish newspaper *Jyllands-Posten* in 2005.[14]

First, as a general comment, I think that it is already problematic to discuss this issue on the basis of blasphemy and free
speech as primary oppositional parameters. For this, Mahmood

---

14. Saba Mahmood, "Religious Reason and Secular Affect: An Incom-
mensurable Divide?," in *Is Critique Secular? Blasphemy, Injury, and Free
Speech* (Berkeley, Calif.: Townsend Center for the Humanities, 2009), 64–
100. Hereafter cited in the text. The volume includes an essay by Talal Asad,
a response by Judith Butler, and an introduction by Wendy Brown.

and Asad, as well as Judith Butler, who responds to both of them in the discussion, are not directly culpable; this is how the entire controversy is articulated by dominant discourses on both sides. Yet this very fact deserves to be questioned. To think of this case in terms of blasphemy versus free speech is already to capitulate to the established order of the religion versus secularism debate. "Blasphemy" in its original Greek literally means harm induced by words. I will come back to the significance of words in a minute, but let us first consider the issue of harm. Harm to whom? Who is the injured figure? Any response that does not serve some sort of orthodoxy would state the obvious: Injury is induced against real human beings. It is utterly absurd to consider that the injured party is the Prophet or God himself, or any particular religion in the abstract, even if we flatter ourselves that we can inhabit a wholly metaphorical landscape. Yet charges of blasphemy have always been considered in terms of assault on the divine. The brutal fact of the matter, in this particular case, is that the blasphemous gesture of the Danish cartoons was motivated by unadulterated racism. The cartoon image of the Prophet as terrorist is nothing more than a gloss on the Arab as quintessential terrorist, as Edward Said tirelessly pointed out for decades. The social, ethnic, and cultural differences among Muslims are entirely disregarded here; the signifier "Muslim" is a gloss of the signifier "Arab" that preceded it. This is classic Orientalism. The terrorist is a racialized figure, and the injury of the cartoons is no different than injury produced by racist hate speech. On this basis alone the counterargument collapses because the free-speech defense becomes irrelevant: freedom of speech cannot be invoked to protect racist injurious speech any more than it can protect an act of murder.

More subtle and certainly undiscussed in this whole debate remains the other dimension of how and why this problem was conceptualized as injury by words (blasphemy). To remain ensnared in the problematic of words is all the more curious given that the controversy pertains to images. The unexamined ease with which images give themselves up to the power of words while words are denied their own imagistic register is one of the core problems of the case. The discourses of both religion and secularism are equally complicit in this problem and remain, moreover, entirely unreflexive about their mutual mirroring or, worse yet, about their coming together in battle against each other over their own mirrored sacred spaces. A perfect illustration of this complicity is the celebrated case in Russia in the summer of 2012, when the punk feminist group Pussy Riot was condemned for blasphemy against religion by a secular state that was the target of the group's secular (needless to say) critique. To say that the state operated here as a sacred entity is to (over)state the obvious.[15]

It is commendable that Mahmood attempts to work beyond the quandary between images and words by focusing on the affective register of the image, making expressive use of W. J. T. Mitchell's argument about excising the analysis of images from the analysis of language.[16] But her apt use of Mitchell is

15. As the case became the newest commodity issue for media worldwide, the barrage of commentary not only by pundits but also by academics and intellectuals was put to shame by the women's own words in their closing statements at the trial. For, quite beyond the fashionable language of freedom of speech versus blasphemy, the women spelled out the crux of the case to be the utterly cynical complicity between the secularist and the religious elements of the Russian political status quo. It was against this cynical opportunism that Pussy Riot acted and on whose authority its members were condemned. The closing statements deserve a close reading and an essay of their own, but in fact they speak brilliantly for themselves. See the translated texts in the Summer 2012 issue of *N+1*, accessed on its website, http://npluso nemag.com/pussy-riot-closing-statements.

16. W. J. T. Mitchell, *What Do Images Want? The Lives and Loves of Images* (Chicago: University of Chicago Press, 2005). However, it does not seem that Mahmood would have much use for Mitchell's notion of "critical idolatry," which is perfectly apt in the situation of the Danish cartoons, because she cannot imagine in what sense the investment of certain Muslims in the unrepresentability of the image of Muhammad—and therefore the sense of injury at its depiction—is an idolatrous investment. See Mitchell's interesting

still haunted by the same presumption that structures *Politics of Piety* and her work after it: that the realm of the sacred is beyond identitary semiotics, and that in this case images derive their meaning from a complex ritual/devotional relation to sacred practices and affects. Mahmood curiously restricts the semiotic to material (secular) objects—the image qua image—as if the nonmaterial (nonsecular), even as pure relation, can ever escape semiosis. I would certainly concur with her critique of the secularist tendency to disengage imagistic representation from sacred devotion in the name of a general critique of the inadequacy of representation as an interpretive rubric for the realm of images. However, the problem with sacred images is not what they represent, whether to devotees or infidels who mock them. It is what they signify through precisely the relation they set in effect, the specific semantics of this relation.

Mahmood insightfully draws from the history of the meaning of the icon in order to stage her argument: "*Icon* refers not only to an image but to a cluster of meanings that might suggest a persona, an authoritative presence, or even a shared imagination. . . . The term *icon* in my discussion therefore pertains not just to images but to a form of relationality that binds the subject to an object or imaginary" (74). It is precisely this relationality that I am also interested in, although I cannot just ignore the ease with which the verb "bind" is used here without question, and how indeed it qualifies the relational field as a one-way street. Things become more problematic with the needless recourse to Aristotle, which is, moreover, ill informed. Mahmood attempts to bolster her argument with reference to the alleged Aristotelian notion of *schesis* (simply speaking, relation), with specific reference to Aristotle's *Categories*. The fact is that Aristotle does not quite use this word; his term for relation is *pros ti*, which literally designates the proximity of two things,

---

and succinct formulation of what he means by this term at http://d13.documenta .de/#/research/research/view/on-critical-idolatry.

of one thing tending toward another and, by inference, coming into relation. The primary meaning of the word *schesis*, which is derived from the verb *schein* or *echein* (to have), pertains to state or condition, often in reference to the body; hence its cognate relation to *hexis* (habit), which Mahmood duly mentions, but inaccurately: "both [*schesis* and *hexis*] suggesting a bodily condition or temperament that undergirds a particular modality of relation" (76). Except in exactly opposite ways: while *schesis* means a temporary or passing, and therefore alterable, condition—Aristotle categorizes relation among the accidents, the contingent relation of beings (*Cat.* 6a36–7b14)—*hexis* indeed means temperament and therefore a permanent condition. This is a crucial misstep because surely Mahmood would never want the sacred relation of Muslims to Muhammad to be a temporary condition or a passing fancy.[17]

The historical record of the use of the word *schesis* philosophically has nothing to do with Aristotle. It is imputed to Aristotelianism by subsequent commentators, initially the Stoics, but most important, it is taken up in early Patristic texts, especially by Gregory of Nyssa (ca. 335–ca. 394), whose philosophy of language, deriving but ultimately dissenting from

---

17. Mahmood makes another hasty association between the Aristotelian notion of ethical virtue (*aretē*) and the Islamic tradition of piety (96n21). This is a manufactured association. There is no piety in Aristotle or anywhere in classical Greek philosophy. Piety is a Christian notion, and whatever its Islamic significance may be, it needs to be traced through that trajectory. More important, Aristotelian virtue may be identified as *hexis* (temperament, habitus), which is presumably why Mahmood makes the association, but significantly as *hexis proairetikē* (*Nicomachean Ethics* II.6.1107a), that is, as an optional temperament, determined by one's *phronēsis*. Of course, optional temperament is, strictly speaking, a contradiction in terms. But this is precisely the crux not only of the Aristotelian ethos but also of the Greek social imaginary as such. One's ethical practice is never a mere application of rules, but an autonomous exercise born through interrogative self-reflection and critique (*phronēsis*). One might go so far as to say that this ethical practice is precisely (self-) critique, but obviously not in a Kantian sense.

basic Neoplatonist concepts, was essential in arguing through the logical contradictions of Trinitarian consubstantiality.[18] A continuation of a line of argument on the basis of relational hypostasis reaches to the era of Byzantine iconophilia, which Mahmood duly mentions, even if via a skewed genealogy. It may enter Islamic thought perhaps through glosses on Aristotelian thinking or by theological assimilation generally within the Abrahamic religious tradition—this I am not prepared to evaluate—but in essence it has nothing to do with Greek philosophy; it is theological through and through, from Orthodox to Roman Christianity to, perhaps, Islam; at least, this is Mahmood's argument in reference to Muslim practices all the way to the contemporary world. The gist of the argument is what matters:

> The point I wish to emphasize is that, within traditions of Muslim piety, a devout relationship to Muhammad is predicated not so much on a communicative or representational model as on an assimilative one. Muhammad, in this understanding, is not simply a proper noun referring to a particular historical figure, but the mark of a relation of similitude. In this economy of signification, he is a figure of immanence in his constant exemplariness and is therefore not a referential sign that stands apart from an essence that it denotes. (76)

And later:

> For many pious Muslims, these embodied practices and virtues provide the substrate through which one comes to acquire a devoted and pious disposition. Such an inhabitation of the model (as the term *schesis* suggests) is the result of a labor of love in which one is bound to the authorial figure through a sense of intimacy and desire. It is not due to the compulsion of "the law" that one emulates the Prophet's conduct, therefore, but because of the ethical

18. See Luca F. Mateo Seco and Gulio Maspero, eds., *The Brill Dictionary of Gregory of Nyssa* (Leiden: Brill, 2009), especially the entries on Aristotle, hypostasis, and philosophy of language.

capacities one has developed that incline one to behave in a certain way. (77–78)

That *schesis* does not at all mean or suggest inhabitation is not the issue here. Mahmood wants to argue for a certain kind of embodied relationality that exceeds both the strict parameters of self (as understood in the Cartesian tradition) and a representational framework of authority in favor of emulation of exemplarity. In this situation, pure imagistic depiction is not only alien to the devotional context; it is injurious, in an altogether real sense, to the devout person.

I do not dispute this description of injury at all, much as I cannot dispute—who could?—the profoundly embodied affective relation between human beings and their modes of faith.[19] Marx himself, in the most celebrated radical critique of religion, described religion as the self-esteem (*Selbstgefühl*) of humanity—literally, the affect of self. But my agreement derives from an altogether different standpoint, which Mahmood unwittingly confirms. I cannot imagine that she would perceive it this way, but her analysis falls right into the problematic of idolatry, which is inherent in all religious worship even if it is denied. What Mahmood describes as the devout relation between God and the faithful exemplifies the full affective investment that forms religious sentiment as such, in which all aspects of the sacred, even words themselves—perhaps especially words or even cognitive abstractions (e.g., the Trinity, the unpronounceable name of God, the Unrepresentable)—function as pure objects of worship (*latreia*), as idols. This is

19. On the other hand, the charge of injury or pain in itself is not a cognitive category for comparative anthropological research. Pain can never be measured and certainly cannot be compared. This is also pointed out, among a whole lot of other things, in the most intelligent and thorough reading of Mahmood's essay, Andrew March's "Speaking about Muhammad, Speaking about Muslims," *Critical Inquiry* 37, no. 4 (Summer 2011): 806–21.

the radical meaning of Cornelius Castoriadis's phrase "Every religion is idolatry": it is not what an image represents but what it signifies that enables it to be an object of worship or devotion, which is why it exceeds the divide between the visual and the sayable.[20] In this sense, unlike how Mahmood perceives it—or rather, in different terms than she means it—modes of worship and devotion, in their ritual embodied practice, are fully engaged in semiosis to the extent that they enact a specific semantics, a mode of production of societal meaning that they inscribe in a variety of ways and means, in texts and on bodies.

To argue that "ethical capacities" of the faithful via emulation of divine example are due not to obedience to the law but to customary practices that emerge and are reinforced by ritual does not outmaneuver the heteronomous nature of the relation. "The notion of moral injury I am describing . . . emanates not from the judgment that 'the law' has been transgressed but from the perception that one's being, *grounded as it is in a relationship of dependency with the Prophet,* has been shaken. . . . The offense the cartoons committed was not against a moral interdiction, but against a structure of affect, a habitus, that feels wounded" (78; my emphasis). Law does not need to be a written command, although there are plenty of those, and all monotheistic religions share them prominently. There is law just as well in a practice initiated by an Other (or in the name of an Other) who remains unquestioned and cannot even be depicted, an Other whose example leads the way and on whom one is dependent. A traditional habitus is not absolved of ideological identification, or subjugation in certain instances. It signifies a mode by which a community is bound together, and

20. See Cornelius Castoriadis, "Institution of Society and Religion," in *World in Fragments: Writings on Politics, Society, Psychoanalysis, and the Imagination,* ed. David Ames Curtis (Stanford, Calif.: Stanford University Press, 1997), 325. I discuss this essay and this issue at length in "Idolatry, Prohibition, Unrepresentability," *boundary 2* 40, no. 1 (Winter 2013), 137–55.

in this respect it very well carries both a semiotic and an identitary function, a function of order.[21]

In being so careful to avoid any suggestion that this embodied relationality is in fact an identitary process that would inevitably demand a critical attitude, Mahmood revokes from her ethnographic subject the capacity to exercise political judgment or even to protect itself against an alien (heteronomous) legal framework. This is the crux of Judith Butler's response to Mahmood as well.[22] Despite the fact that Butler wavers on the issue of whether critique must involve judgment, the demand for the political, which necessitates decision (and, therefore, judgment), cannot be outmaneuvered. The issue is not that the realm of critique (whereby a certain interrogative politics is enacted) bears a secular content. The metaphysics of secularism shows perfectly well how critique can be dissolved in the pursuit of certain ideological interests. Rather, the issue is that

---

21. It is also careless to discount in what sense this affective habitus that safeguards an order of things is in fact vulnerable to manipulation and provocation by external agents that mean to do it harm by mobilizing precisely the vehemence of devotional affect. This is the lesson of the widespread protests in the Islamic world as a result of the outrageous film denigrating Muhammad that surfaced on the Internet in September 2012. Whoever was indeed behind this deliberately hideous production consciously acted as a provocateur, exploiting a community's uninterrogated affect in order to destabilize the order that this affect allegedly ensures. The murky rumor mill around the arrested filmmaker, as well as the presumed financing (it is preposterous to consider that $5 million was raised for this ridiculously low-budget fragment of film unless we are talking of a Ponzi scheme), testifies to the high probability of maleficent provocation. Denouncing the criminal intent of the filmmakers and producers goes without saying, but what deserves critical attention is the lack of self-interrogation of the faithful, who thereby become all the more vulnerable to injury, manipulation, and subjugation to external power.

22. Judith Butler, "The Sensibility of Critique: A Response to Asad and Mahmood," in *Is Critique Secular? Blasphemy, Injury, and Free Speech* (Berkeley, Calif.: Townsend Center for the Humanities, 2009), 101–36.

regardless of content (religious, secular, or what have you), the interrogative politics of critique forms the domain of the secular simply in the sense that it entails a worldly enactment.

Practices of interrogative critique may be said to be the persistent condition of the secular even if the precise content of how they are conducted is itself conditioned by pertinent social-historical realities, and even if the language in which they are conducted is the language of religion. Embodiment, affect, ritual, etc., are as much materialities of the secular as of any other domain. There is nothing more misguided than identifying the critical-in-the-secular with the rational or the disembodied. The kind of statement that Mahmood makes that "unlike religious belief, critique is predicated upon a necessary distantiation between the subject and the object and some form of reasoned deliberation" (90) is baffling to me, as are claims that secularism obliterates the visceral element in human mindfulness—this is in part William Connolly's claim in *Why I Am Not a Secularist* (1999). In her response, Butler insightfully foregrounds Foucault's reconfiguration of Kantian reason as an attitude and an ethos that certainly involves corporeal and affective involvement in communal situations, yet cognizant of the antagonistic terrain of relations. A critical attitude cannot consist in giving oneself over to the given. For a critical attitude, both the sacred and the profane are given only in that they denote certain social-historical realities, and all such realities, as human creations under specific conditions, are subject to inquiry, evaluation, and perhaps alteration should this be socially decided. Even here, a critical attitude entails involvement in such social decisions as self-cognizant action in an antagonistic sphere, where nothing can be said to be determined in advance or by some sort of extrasocial principle residing outside the field of contention. This is why critique is always political in a profoundly democratic sense, and why it inhabits the domain of *doxa*, not *dogma*, and certainly not *logos* as it has come to be understood. As engagement with *doxa*, critique shows that despite its uses in all kinds of cultural grammars, orthodoxy is a nonsensical notion, a contradiction in terms.

To the extent that it is predicated on (self-)critique, secular praxis cannot obliterate antagonism in favor of a set value structure and cannot claim to reside beyond the murky vicissitudes of affect in order to uphold the crystal symmetry of an a priori validating order. If we take seriously the etymology of the word (*saeculum* in Latin being roughly equivalent to the Greek-derived *epoch*), what resides at its core is the notion of time—indeed, even the notion of the spirit of the times, the era of things. *Saeculum* is an archaic rendering of what in modernity we denote as *Zeitgeist* without troubling ourselves with the fact that the spirit is subjected to the order of time or that it gains its power because of the order of time—not the other way around. From this standpoint, the secular is in a direct and simple sense the historical and in that respect the worldly: simply, the domain that human beings define by means of their action in their finite life. Thus, in the same direct and simple sense, any rejection of the secular is a rejection of history, of the (self-)making and unmaking of human life as something preciously finite in a finite world.

This line of argument would recognize that the denial of the secular, even if in the most otherworldly terms, is actually part of the domain of the secular insofar as it aims to affect or alter the real conditions of human life. This is why I find the classic antinomy between the secular and the religious inaccurate. Insofar as religion is a social practice, a mode of ritual communal binding, its significance is a secular matter, and theological concerns (like philosophical ones), from this standpoint, belong to the necessary practices by which humanity encounters the enigma of its existence. This is why I argue, bluntly, that the ultimate point is not merely to disrupt the antinomic complicity between the religious and the secular but to take away from the religious the agency of determining what is secular.

I understand how one could protest that this position is already rigged because it takes for granted the secularist explanation of the world, in which, according to the standard thesis, the very separation between the secular and the religious, the worldly and the otherworldly, is made possible. I understand the explanation that this separation was produced historically by conditions recognized to belong to the "Christian West" (thus hardly natural), which led to the advent and, later, the imposition of secularism as an institutional framework of social existence: secularism representing the globalized expansion of an institutional ideology. I don't dispute such arguments. No doubt, secular institutions have emerged as part of the history of the Christian West, and certainly, secularism has been very much part of the "civilizing mission" of the colonialist project—although not in a way more capacious than overt Christianization of colonized peoples by armies of missionaries. And one can surely charge that this historically produced separation between religious and secular realms presupposes my argument. Yet I have not seen a cogent epistemological argument for what usefulness the undifferentiated complicity between these two realms might provide. History shows that what precedes this acknowledged separation between the religious and the secular—at least, in the monotheistic world—is a condition whereby the religious occupies the totality of social meaning. This condition, in my terms, simply marks the incapacity of society to articulate the obvious: that social meaning is always a historical creation by men and women under specific living conditions, and that in this respect, even theocracy is a worldly regime—it takes place in history; indeed, it *produces* history.

The work that engages with the nebulous epistemology of worldly practices is the work of secular criticism, as Edward Said argued consistently from the earliest phases of his thinking. Although Said never theorized this notion outside a specific literary domain, a careful reading of his multifarious body of work demonstrates that secular criticism marks a terrain of thought and action that, as an open-ended interrogative encounter with the world, not only disdains but uncompromisingly subverts, battles, and outdoes any sort of transcendentalist condition for resolving social and historical problems. In the most direct sense, secular criticism purports to unmask social historical situations where authority is assumed to emerge from *elsewhere*. This, I repeat, includes the metaphysics of secularism. At this time, when the disparate variants of antisecularist thinking converge in yet another mode of heteronomous politics, detranscendentalizing the secular is, as far as I am concerned, the most urgent task of secular criticism.

THREE

Why I Am Not a Post-secularist

I am not a post-secularist because I am not even a secularist. I am an atheist.

Of these three presumed identifications, the last is the crucial one, if only because it resists the logic of identity, despite the explicit subjective affirmation ("I am"). Saying this, I understand, aggravates the already-peculiar syllogism I am positing, which to some could appear sophistic.

In the conventional sense, the phenomenon of atheism belongs to the history of secularization and may even be the apogee of secular imagination. However, recent thinking on this issue, from Talal Asad's *Genealogies of Religion* (1993) onward, would correct this convention by specifically arguing that atheism is but an extension of the Christian imagination and thereby carries—perhaps even exemplifies—Christianity's significations, even if in another language. Another beacon of this position, conducted differently from Asad's, is Marcel Gauchet's argument in *The Disenchantment of the World* (1985). This tendency has been offered as an indication of and has been celebrated as (while celebrating in turn) the advent of an era that

has been named "post-secularist." The genealogy of this naming is complex and has not yet been written. At a basic level,
however, we can say that the name "post-secularism" exhibits
the worst of all "post" designations: generally, a lazy way of codi-
fying emergent historical terrains. The facile and proliferating
nomenclature of all kinds of "post" somethings bears with it
the incapacitated response to the emergent and is thereby an
already-defeated designation. Certainly, it testifies to the impoverishment of the terms of discussion of contemporary problems and undermines whatever might be genuine efforts to think
otherwise.

The term "post-secular" is particularly nonsensical to me.
(So is the term "post-political," but that's another issue.) In order to have any rigor at all, "post-secular" would have to mean
either that some sort of pure secularity has been achieved—
that the so-called process of secularization has been completed—or that the secular has been left behind, outmaneuvered
or indeed abolished by another social-imaginary horizon. We
know that entertaining the first possibility is absurd under any
account of present history; besides, as I have argued, secularization is unfinishable by its very terms as a historical project.
If the second were indeed true, then what is the condition to
which we have now newly arrived? Let's give it a name. We
don't want to say "religiosity" or even "religion" as such—in
whatever form religion might be incarnated in various languages. First, again on the simple basis of the present historical
record, we have never left the world of religion—one cannot
leave a world except by dying, and religion is still living. Second, we claim to want to deconstruct the word "religion," and,
in any case, we object to the simplistic ideological notion of the
so-called resurgence of religion. But, at the same time, we do
not want to resort to the name "secular," but we invoke it with
the generic prefix that, as if by some inordinate magic, renames
it in the very claim to have made it vanish. These are regrettable
contortions. To call our present historical moment "post-secular"
is testimony to our incapacity to deconstruct the secular. One

of the reasons—not the only one—is precisely the unwillingness to confront secular criticism as an experimental and (self-)
interrogative engagement with the social-historical, or, even
more, as a *poiêtic* encounter with the social imaginary of our
times. Instead, we confound secular criticism with the institution of secularism, whose metaphysics we conveniently identify
as the new theology, and, washing our hands of the latter (for
who would dare deconstruct theology anymore?), we settle
comfortably in the armchair of the post-secular.

I have obviously engaged in a catachrestic use of "we," for I
don't think there is any way to absolve oneself—if one wants to
claim having anything to say on this matter—from complicity
with/in the secular.

Against this newly achieved comfort, I have been proposing
that one of the key tropes of secular criticism is to detranscendentalize the secular, precisely so as not to get bogged down in
such simple equations between the secular and the theological.
The disjunction between the secular and the theological owes
itself, first of all, to the fact of the "failure" of secularization, or
perhaps more accurately, the incompleteness of secularization.
The point is not to explore in what ways secularization can be
completed. The aspiration for completion is itself dictated by
a theological desire. Something more modest is at stake, a historical claim. Secularization is of consequence precisely as a
disruption of the Christian apocalyptic trajectory and, by extension, any apocalyptic trajectory. It is a reorientation of the
social imagination toward the validation of the finitude of life
(mortality) over total finitude (rapture) and, conversely, the validation of the infinite possibility of human invention over its
restricted condition in the finality of the All-Signifying God—or,
frankly, any all-signifying entity. This reorientation, expressly
constituted against the monotheistic imaginary that eventually
becomes globally dominant, is always partial. Curiously, I
would argue, the metaphysics of secularism is an outcome of
this partial turn, of this constitutive incompleteness, precisely as
the remainder of the totalizing desire for completion. If secular

criticism takes to task secularist metaphysics, it cannot stay at the facile level of merely identifying theological remainders in a secular age. Moreover, if (and that is not a necessary "if") secular criticism would see it as its task to focus on a possible structural equation between secularism and religion—this has become the dominant paradigm of the post-secular—it would mean to subject both, equally and simultaneously, to relentless dismantling.

For this reason, yet again, it is an error to disavow the difference between secularism and secular criticism. The two cannot be equated, I repeat, because at the very least, as an institutional metaphysics, secularism is one of the objects taken to task by secular criticism. The self-interrogative focus of secular criticism is not on how religion is secularized but on how society is (to be) desacralized. It is in this specific context of interrogation that I invoke atheism as a point of departure.

For the sake of argument, permit me to make certain assertions. I will not, for the purposes of this argument, contextualize my position in the course of the history of atheism; this is reserved for a later and longer piece of writing.

My position cannot be further away from both currently fashionable rationalist-naturalist atheism (espoused by the likes of Richard Dawkins or Sam Harris) and the Christian-derived atheism of nonbelief. I understand that for so-called post-secularists the first is mere conjuring of the second in scientistic language. However, we need to hold on to this distinction so as not to fall into the epistemological collapse that sees religion everywhere and in everything secular. Christian-derived atheism may be said to be distilled in the declaration "I don't believe in God" or "I don't believe there is a God." This statement amounts to self-delusion insofar as it refuses to acknowledge that the negation it claims participates in the terminological framework of belief, a discourse that, from the standpoint of religious conviction, belongs to the epistemology of God. To paraphrase Jacqueline Rose, the specter of unbelievability is not a threat to belief; it belongs squarely to its signifying horizon. I call this atheism "Christian-derived" in order to accentuate that it is inevitably marked by the condition of "God is dead" in its Nietzschean declaration, the trauma of which, nonetheless, does not break down the necessity for belief. On the contrary, it reiterates and preserves, albeit by denying it, the semantics of belief as a prosthetic dependency, as an existential justification on whose crutch the debilitating encounter with the abyss of the world is allegedly yet again overcome.

An atheism that will have emancipated itself from Christianity would render the matter of belief or nonbelief in God irrelevant or, more significantly, would recognize it as a matter of performance. In saying this, I am suggesting an all-out interrogation of transcendental authority that would hinge on how one can perform one's worldly existence without God, not out of some sort of conviction, of belief in unbelief, but as a performance of a fact that eschews conviction, a performance of a fact that requires no demonstration or verification. This performance is always ephemeral, if nothing else because its object is groundless. It has to be constantly reperformed, each time anew, discontinuously even if constantly, repeated in utter singularity, untimely, ungrounded. The reality of this performance resides in its virtuality. Such real-virtual atheism would not be deconstructible; it is certainly not reducible to a convenient pretension, comfort zone, or conventional cynicism. Instead, it would stake out a position of living without presuming a content for the void of the Real, of living by assuming the void as core with no need to justify it, explain it, or theorize it—without a need for a transcendental, metaperformative guarantee.

This radical performative (real-virtual) atheism would leave Christianity and all its social-imaginary mechanisms behind. It would mean to live not as if God does not exist but to live as if God does not matter. What does this mean? At the most elemental level, it means that I live my life unconcerned with whether people around me believe or don't believe in divinity. Unconcerned certainly does not mean oblivious, contemptuous, or disapproving. It means divested, disinterested. Perhaps

we can even say indifferent, in the sense that this position bears
a certain philosophical weight since the Stoics: certain things
in life are *adiaphora*, that is, indifferent (literally speaking, not
delimited) and thus unsusceptible to the righteous limitations
of morality. I am not addressing here the significance this term
took in post-Reformation theology to refer to matters that are
neither commanded nor prohibited by God, except to note that
in this context the term specified a secular space of freedom
from the permutations of belief, indeed, a space in-between the
polarities of belief, as Michel de Certeau has argued succinctly:
"Belief occurs in the recognition of an alterity and the estab-
lishment of a contract."[1] Certainly, to take seriously the notion
of contract is to reiterate the economics intrinsic to the language of belief; to believe (*credo*) is to engage in a credit investment, for you extend yourself out on a limb without necessarily
possessing the proper resources. Likewise—and that is the
other side of the polarity—you have extended yourself beyond
the reach of your present resources into an alien terrain, which
you can encounter only on the basis of some sort of established
credibility. Both standpoints, alterity and contract, are entwined on the basis of trust, yet another word that enacts the
economic (and eventually theological) ethics of belief. I am
merely following here de Certeau's impeccable semiological
orchestration of a Latin verb that emerges from a classic Roman entwinement of the economic with the juridical and
passes into the dominant Christian theology that inherits it.

Permit me here a brief philological digression. It is interesting, for the sake of argument, but also because it resonates
directly with the foray into the tragic, as sketched later, that
corresponding to the Latin *credo*, as the matrix of the signification of believing, is the Greek *nomizein*, which bears an alto-

---

1. Michel de Certeau, "What Do We Do When We Believe?," in *On
Signs*, ed. Marshall Blonsky (Baltimore: Johns Hopkins University Press,
1985), 192–202. This essay remains, to my mind, the consummate meditation
on the notion of belief etymologically, historically, and philosophically.

gether different social-imaginary investment, even when it too, at some point, involves the economic (*nomisma* means both coin and what one believes). But the difference is on what, in a modern language, we would call the juridical plane. The Greek verb is obviously derived from *nomos* (law), but *nomos* comes to mean law from the initial significance of *nemein*—apportioning, dividing, delimiting, but also, sharing with others (having a share [*nomē*], a part of some whole divided among many, most obviously land at some inaugural level) and thereby having a place, inhabiting a piece of land for cultivation and thus residence. (A nomad is a person who makes a home wherever his inhabitance of the land will produce a proper share of sustenance.) From Pindar's era onward, the use of the verb *nomizein* indicates believing in the sense of having a particular point of view (its synonymity with having a theory, *theorein*, has been amply pointed out), a share of knowledge, often along the lines of a custom (*nomimon*), as when Antigone famously invokes *agrapta nomima* (unwritten laws, customs) against Creon's decreed law. Even the economic signification of *nomisma* (coin) initially means something assumed by custom (as in Aeschylus's *Persians*, for example), believed by convention, agreement, etc.—precisely what any monetary currency would be for any society.[2] Contrary to *nomizein*, the verb *pisteuein*, to which the early Christians match the Roman *credo* (*pistis* in New Testament Greek means "faith") is a much later development. In Plato's *Apology*, Socrates often uses the phrase *theous nomizein* ("believing in the gods"), never *theous pisteuein*. This later development alters the entire framework of meaning. *Pistis* does not stand for belief as point of view or even trust in one's own opinion, but rather for knowing the true (following the permutations of Platonism), an entirely different construction of language that essentially maps the passage from *doxa* to *dogma*, which is

2. This etymological trajectory is discussed at length in the context of the Greek political imaginary in Cornelius Castoriadis's *Thucydide, la force et le droit* (Paris: Seuil, 2011), 297–300.

in effect the passage from the Greek to the Christian imaginary. Dogma can never be indifferent by definition, but *doxa* is constituted precisely by the sort of belief that is attached to nothing other than the risk of opinion in the shared, but contentious, realm of the opinions of others.

To return to my argument, the freedom of indifference—*adiaphoron*—is not only a gesture against a dogmatic investment in the truth of God; it also means to be unconcerned with—or unsusceptible to—the Nietzschean proposition that "God is dead." Those who still labor under the Nietzschean predicament assume, whether in cognizance or not, that there was a time when God was alive. The assumption that affirms divine existence, even if it has now lapsed, participates in the same imaginary that authorizes certain devout believers to confess that God speaks to them directly. Living as if God is dead is merely the end point in a continuous spectrum of belief. To reiterate de Certeau's terms, which address explicitly the Christian imaginary, the recognition of alterity remains, and the contract is reestablished, this time with the conviction of unbelief.

The death of God is a Christian proposition; the irrelevance of God, the void, is not. Christianity is the first (and so far only) religion to be founded on the altogether perverse notion of killing God. The emphasis is on foundation. None of the numerous myths that comprise, say, the Ovidian inventory of metamorphoses of gods dying and being reborn are applicable in this sense. The death of Osiris, to think of a specific example, is not a foundational act, and the fact that he is conventionally considered to be a prototype for Christ is conceivable only in a Christian – and Christian-derived – imagination. Of course, access to knowledge of this perversion is barred from the founding moment because in Christianity the killing of God is neither gratuitous nor an act of rebellion. God is put to death precisely to claim conquest over death. The death of God in Christianity is thus marked by uncompromising instrumentality. God dies so that he may be resurrected, simple as that.

The instrumental outcome is all that matters (the abolition of sin happens with the Resurrection, not the Crucifixion), and the reality of God's death—*God's suicide*, to be exact—vanishes behind the interminable ritual repetition of a mythical spectacle rendered sacred. The ontological status of the Christian God, therefore, is somewhat like the living dead, the Undead, like one of those astounding monsters in horror movies. It is hardly surprising that such creatures in movies are inevitably associated at some point with something satanic—the singularity of the satanic being the Christian invention of God's other side.

In retrospect, after two millennia, it seems that the death of God in Christianity was meant to abolish once and for all the possibility that God might be rendered truly irrelevant to our existence, that God might be voided. It is a mark of humanity's ultimately untamable psychic core that this imaginary possibility has still not been extinguished. Nietzsche's "death of God" may be considered, on the one hand, the final act of Christian thinking, but, on the other hand, it may be the first act of un-Christian thinking from within because it also signaled the death of the Resurrection and a return to life as actualization of mortality. Living with a sense of utter mortality, of plain finitude, diminishes the hold of death over life. If death is zero, then all life before it curiously becomes infinity and plenitude in every infinitesimal, ephemeral, and unreproducible moment. If the zero of death is undone by the promise of an eternal afterlife, a promise that turns infinity itself into a promise, then death's zero expands backward all over life and, like a radioactive cloud, envelops it and removes from it all temporality. It annihilates its (life) force and hollows it out into a perfunctory shell yearning to be filled with promise.

To live as if God does not matter in full cognizance of annihilating mortality, therefore, is to live in ways that cannot be measured in the spectrum of belief, in ways that cannot be measured at all. It is to make a wager, but quite unlike Pascal's

skepticism as it is often reproduced in the popular imagination: Believe in God because you've got nothing to lose; if he
exists, you will be rewarded, and if he doesn't, it won't matter.
Instead, the wager carries a greater risk: Be unconcerned with
the divine. Be concerned, show compassion, care for what is
human, even if what is human is often abominable. Dogmatic
believers would counter with the warning that such pronounce-
ments bring on me the full force of divine wrath, the loss of
eternal bliss. But if I care only for this life, this one fragile, inadequate, ephemeral, but oh so precious, small life, in the
midst of other equally inadequate and precious small lives,
where is the loss? Even if I may grant that there is a loss, it is
irrelevant. If I have chosen to reside fully in the incalculable,
surely I do not need to calculate how many chips it takes to
enter Paradise.

It goes without saying that an argument about the irrelevance of the divine cannot be conducted neutrally as a moral,
philosophical, or scientific argument; it is embedded in the
performative politics of worldliness. This is a politics conscious of making history only for the sake of history, in full
cognizance that as history, it is condemned to be overwritten,
overturned, overtaken. To borrow a phrase from Sadia Abbas,
worldliness cannot turn history into theodicy—this would be
its demise. A succinct moment of such atheist performativity is
Woody Allen's quip in *Stardust Memories* (1980), where his character responds to the accusation of being an atheist with "To
you, I am an atheist. To God, I am the loyal opposition." Such
performative politics renders belief or unbelief in God immaterial, much as it renders the question of God's existence or nonexistence irrelevant. More significantly, it thereby exposes that
both discourses (belief and unbelief) consist in producing an
authority materialized out of the immaterial, which occludes
the encounter with worldly things that really matter. It may be
that instead of speaking of belief, we should speak of idolatry.
Let's put idolatry in the place of belief or unbelief in our conceptual vocabulary and see what happens!

There is no way in which the issue can be resolved by taking cover behind some sort of noncommittal agnosticism: "I don't really know whether God exists, so I withdraw judgment in the matter." One counters this with Ludwig Wittgenstein's assertion that the strictly agnostic position is impossible. I cannot presume not to know with the certainty of knowledge. In Wittgenstein's (sense of) language, I cannot say, "I know that I don't know," Socrates notwithstanding, without compromising the radical power of nonknowledge, which obviously has nothing to do with ignorance. I cannot presume not to know because I would have to imagine (therefore, know) what it is I do not or cannot know. Interestingly, despite his celebrated claim of knowing only the fact that he does not know anything, in the *Apology* Socrates makes an argument about not knowing death that bears similar elements to Wittgenstein's: namely, one cannot possibly fear death, for this would mean that one would know what cannot be known (29a.6–9). The common premise here is that one cannot act on what one does not know. In these terms, a dogmatic atheism, according to which God's nonexistence would be positively proposed, would entail a self-defeating principle, entirely self-enclosed in the regime of belief in the name of unbelief. Indeed, a dogmatic atheism assumes that it can speak of God's nonexistence as a transcendental position, that is, as if this nonexistence exists beyond the world. And, in Wittgenstein's language, "The world is all that is the case."[3]

What's left, then? To encounter the Wittgensteinian demand seriously would mean to perform atheism without the least necessity, desire, or investment in its truth—to be an atheist without the least concern to prove the validity of its meaning. (This is precisely where I part from the rationalist atheism of Richard

3. In developing this point, I gained immensely from discussions with Aristides Baltas and from his new book *Peeling Potatoes or Grinding Lenses: Spinoza and the Young Wittgenstein Converse on Immanence and Its Logic* (Pittsburgh: Pittsburgh University Press, 2012).

Dawkins, Sam Harris, or Christopher Hitchens.) But why
should one perform at all in this context, especially if one re-
jects the appeal to "reason" (or, in this case, secularism) as another instance of transcendentalist metaphysics? Apart from
the strategic answer that pertains to a specific politics that
seeks to counter the globality of religious politics, which has
been efficiently disguised in Samuel Huntington's culturalist
language of "the clash of civilizations," the answer involves a
crucial subversive dimension. Living your life by performing
the fact that God does not exist—solely in the sense that God
does not matter, and not because you have a stake in the ontological status of the question whether God is or is not—is to
destabilize any guarantee of providence or destiny. This opens
life to infinite possibility, even if it always puts life at risk.

Such a lack of guarantee in meaning entails, of course, a
tragic condition in altogether extreme terms. In moments of
absolute happiness, of fulfillment, you have to remember—
although this memory will do nothing in itself (as value) to
compromise, subvert, or avert this condition—that such moments may constitute just as well moments of unraveling, of
undoing, and perhaps of destruction. Before you there will always be raised the risk of hubris, but hubris may be the only
legitimate concept (philosophically speaking) of nonknowledge. Like God, hubris cannot be known (until its consequences
are realized), but you must live as though it exists, even though
you don't know it. When even your happiness or your fulfillment may turn out to be a force that generates hubris, you
nonetheless cannot but embrace what you love unequivocally.
But unlike God, hubris is the other to Truth. It is an interpretive horizon about something to be (*à-être*) that is neither a
matter of attending, waiting, or longing for a future to be revealed nor a matter of a transcendent state of immaculate and
immutable Being. When you perform your life in the face of
hubris, you decide not to forget its existence—forgetting hubris is quintessentially hubristic—yet you can do nothing to

suit your existence to its unknown presence. Of the two un-knowables, I decide for hubris over God. Perhaps this is itself the ultimate hubris, one could say. Yes, if hubris is constituted as a transgression of the divine; but not at all, if hubris is a con-dition of the world. All undoing of human existence is a condi-tion of human action and thereby a worldly matter. This is why currently fashionable theories of unmitigated catastrophe as desirable events of radical social-historical transformation—theories seeking a pure aesthetics of catastrophe—are ultimately consumed by theological tropes. In fact, the logic of catastrophe is the inverse of the logic of progress, and both are theological in that they share a reliance on the claim to providence.

In the face of this tragic predicament, of this ever-present *archē* of unraveling, every one of my actions bears the fullest meaning, even the minutest, the most trivial action. Every ac-tion pertains to something incalculable and, therefore, may be the last action, the one that grants final necessity and final meaning to my entire life, the one action that ends my life, the one that gives or ends life for someone else, the one that inter-rupts all that is given, the one that traverses or reverses all ends. This tragic condition entails an irredeemable sadness (we speak of Achilles's wrath in the *Iliad*, but it is his sadness that is sublime), a sadness whose presence persists beneath the greatest and most genuine happiness, even before the moment of real openness to the other. This sadness is not caused by anything external, nor is it resolvable by things external. Thus it is never an obstacle to love, pleasure, or good humor, to the laughter that the *jouissance* of mere existence induces unannounced.

The kind of language I am using commonly generates mis-understanding. Invocations of the tragic produce assump-tions of a dark, ungenerous existence. Nothing could be more contrary. A tragic existence is foremost reliant on a humorous relation to life's adventures, an ironic reception of the abyssal ele-ments of what it means to be, to live, and to die without mean-ing, except for whatever meaning each one of us poetically conjures out of what seems to be nothing but is the groundless nonmeaning of things as such. What in modernist literature was termed the absurdity of existence emerged consistently when and where transcendental repositories of safety had vanished—for whatever reason, this is another question. It is curious that many people recognize that Samuel Beckett is brilliantly tragic in the deepest and most exhilarating moments of his comedic humor, but in invoking images of the tragic in real life, they instantly turn somber and morose, as if they had just violated some ceremonial savoir faire.

My sense is that discourses and practices of belief (including the atheism of belief) denigrate the horizon of decision. Contrary to what seems to be the case—namely, that believers, by virtue of having conviction, are more steadfast in acting, "acting out of conviction," we say, or "acting on our beliefs"—the conditions of belief make all decisions predicate to an originary and binding decision: the decision to believe. The decisions of believers are mere reproductions of decision. That is why they come so easy, if that is what steadfastness is assumed to mean. (Obviously, I'm mocking this assumption; the textual legacies of the trials and tribulations of belief are legion.) But this alleged steadfastness of the believer's decision is a delusion, not in a pathological sense, delusional, but delusionary, because it produces a misperception that you are covered, that you have a transcendental safeguard, when you don't. If decision is to mean anything politically, it must bear the full impact of what Walter Benjamin named "interruption." Let us remember that Benjamin's dialectical mind demands that we understand this interruption not to occur merely in the "external" realm—the hand brake that stops history's runaway train—but internally as well: Every decision is an interruption of the self, an interruption of the given parameters of being.

In contrast, I would argue, the performance of atheism, which produces the condition of permanent disbelief, raises the stakes for the exigency of decision. I mark "disbelief" in its full range of signification: the condition of being in awe before the world, the experience of wonder, the pleasure of discovering that there is always more to discover. Disbelief deconstructs both belief and unbelief, as well as their intrinsic mutually affirming tension. I opt for "disbelief" here in the same way that I opt for "wonder" over "miracle"—in Greek, the word is the same (*thauma*), but it has two radically different meanings before and after the advent of Christianity. The notion of miracle, rendered in New Testament Greek as *thauma*, definitively deprives one of the conscious practice of *thaumazein*—in Aristotle's language, a bona fide philosophical attitude, drawn from the utmost origins of mythical thinking: "For it is owing to wonder [*thaumazein*] that human beings began and continue still to philosophize. . . . And a man who is puzzled [*aporōn*] and wondering [*thaumazōn*] thinks himself ignorant [*oietai agnoein*], whence even the lover of myth is in a sense a lover of wisdom [*philomythos philosophos pōs estin*], for myth is composed of wonders [*o gar mythos sygkeitai ek thaumasiōn*]" (*Metaphysics* 1.982b10–20). The wondrous element that myth articulates, in Aristotle's phrase, emerges from, and never ceases to reside within, a *physis*, no matter how extravagant or extraordinary a *thauma* might seem. Myth is how nature speaks, he tells us, and however enchanting mythical speech may be in itself, its source remains immanent in the wondrous nature of the cosmos itself. Aristotle here returns to a singular characteristic of pre-Socratic naturalist philosophy, which had placed all aspects of the divine or the "supernatural" within, not outside or above, a natural cosmos that exists at the behest of its own lawmaking capacity, in this sense freeing *thauma* from its initial precondition as "the intellectual foundation of magic."[4] In contrast, the subsequent (re)coding of the word *thauma* from wonder to miracle is explicitly made to index whatever contravenes the nature of the cosmos; it is literally

4. See Gregory Vlastos, "Theology and Philosophy in Early Greek Thought," in *Studies in Greek Philosophy*, vol. 1, *The Presocratics* (Princeton: Princeton University Press, 1995), 24.

metaphysical, which is why its (claimed) physical appearance is so otherworldly—the epitome of the otherworldly.

Of course, this does not stop people from investing in the reality of miracles, even when they are entrusted with positions of public responsibility. I remember a few years ago the remarkable comments made publicly by none other than a Supreme Court justice—albeit the Court's most colorful personality, Justice Antonin Scalia—which were posted as instructions to the faithful about how they can resist the malign disregard of the infidel multitude against the glorious reality of Virgin Birth: "It is not irrational to accept the testimony of eyewitnesses who had nothing to gain. There is something wrong with rejecting, a priori, the existence of miracles. . . . If I have brought any message to you today, it is this: Have the courage to have your wisdom regarded as stupidity. Be fools for Christ. And have the courage to suffer the contempt of the sophisticated world."[5] Performing the conventional Orwellian doublespeak of the Bush era, Justice Scalia is unabashedly producing extraordinary syllogisms: "It is irrational not to accept firsthand (i.e., *objective*) accounts of a miracle" and "Have the courage to have your wisdom (i.e., your objective knowledge of miracles) regarded as stupidity by those stupid enough to think themselves sophisticated."

There is no need, I imagine, to elaborate on how another way of registering the meaning of "sophisticated" is to say "worldly." From that standpoint, Scalia's enthusiastic exhortation to "be fools for Christ" (a quotation from 1 Corinthians 4:10) is flaunting the idea "Don't hesitate to be unworldly" or "Don't hesitate to subscribe to the truth—or even more, to the rationality—of the otherworldly." Of course, the fact that all purveyors of doublespeak are caught in their own equivocal logic hardly registers when one espouses stupidity without

---

5. Quoted in James Ridgeway, "Scalia Stumps for Virgin Birth," *Village Voice*, January 25, 2005, 23.

question, especially when stupidity is coded as the way to reason. So the underlying significance of having made the miracle into a worldly category—the matter of disinterested observation, eyewitness testimony at a definite point in history—is conspicuously denied. This double logic merely reverts to its other side. The miraculous is, after all, a self-sufficient category. A miracle is a priori miraculous and, for this reason alone, otherworldly, which is precisely why "the sophisticated world" cannot even remotely entertain its true significance. This is also why it is not only preposterous but patently abject to pursue a scientific explanation of, say, the parting of the Red Sea, as was recently announced by the National Center of Atmospheric Research.

Either Scalia is playing a very sophisticated game of postsecular sophistry—whereby the merging of adversarial epistemologies is meant just to confound those who do rely on worldly modes of thinking and distinguish the miraculous from the realistic—or he is just a robotic vehicle of the ideology he represents: Namely, the miraculous is both in and out of this world, exactly as are the Christian faithful, who can then act in this world in the name of the other world, even if only to wreak havoc on a global scale with the alibi of being ennobled and redeemed in some future apocalyptic moment that will settle all accounts in their favor. Scalia's audience may not know any better, but, insofar as he represents the supreme institution of worldly law in the United States, his illogic is, in fact, a scandal. It is indicative of the scandalous otherworldliness of American politics nowadays that Scalia's invocation of the reality of miracles did not register any scandal, just as George W. Bush's confession that God routinely spoke in his ear did not trigger any alarm in the population that the president was suffering from paranoid episodes.

In earlier and more sophisticated times, as real philosophers keen to address the miracle in philosophical terms, both Spinoza and Hume agreed (with different accounts of its history) that the discourse of the miracle as the contravention of nature is quintessentially religious, having shifted from the signifying framework of magic in polytheism to the signifying framework of divine truth in monotheism. The historical advent of the Christian discourse of the miracle, insofar as it was articulated in the Greek language (*thauma*), obliterated the explicit association in the Greek imaginary between philosophy and myth and thereby inaugurated the desubjectification of one's wondering relation to a wondrous, astonishing, unpredictable world. Because the category of the miracle is self-sufficient, one can be only the object of a miracle, what a miracle acts on by its happening, triggering one's affect as a result of an external effect. One cannot be the subject of a miracle unless one is God, and God is not a subject, at least in the sense of a living being acting and knowing itself acting in the course of time. In any case—and this is the point of Scalia advocating a militant stupidity—one is bedazzled and bereft before a miracle; its experience is perfect heteronomy. The desire for a miracle is a desperate desire—in fact, the desire of desperation par excellence. On the contrary, the experience of *thaumazein*, of responding to the world with a sense of wonder—which is always linked to wondering, to questioning what is given—discredits miracles. Opposite to the effect of the miracle, the effect of wonder happens on your side, on the side of experiencing your *poiein* and your *prattein*, your making and your acting. You induce a sense of wonder in yourself because you remain attuned to the world's wondrous, astonishing fashion—"the bliss of astonishment," says Heidegger. You do not, however, produce the miraculous; the miraculous is revealed to you, generated somehow by an elsewhere as an elsewhere. The miraculous is exceptional because it exempts you, it excludes you. This is why modern theories of "miraculous exception" from Schmitt to Agamben and Badiou are theological theories of exclusionary sovereignty, of heteronomy pure and simple. Regardless of what these theories claim for themselves—that in various ways they exemplify decisionist power—they are the exact opposite: They abrogate the capacity for decision by displacing decision to an undecidable beyond, to a land of miracles. Instead, the uncertainty of wonder, of disbelief (as opposed to the certainty of belief or unbelief), keeps one exceedingly alert to the politics of decision, to the fact that decisions must be made always anew, not because they don't leave a trail or don't need to be consistently followed up, but precisely because their trail must be interrogated and their consistency tested with a sense of wondering.

In this respect, I am advocating a different sort of skepticism: not the condition that by means of interminable negation or constitutive undecidability leads to indecisionism but, on the contrary, the condition that by means of constitutive self-interrogation and radical uncertainty demands precise alertness to the parameters and forces of decision. This obviously presupposes that we learn to be comfortable (or at least unhesitant) in the face of the extraordinary openness of horizon that uncertainty fosters, an openness that requires simultaneously both extremely focused consciousness of the present (as fleeting and ephemeral as it is necessary) and perhaps a mad investment in the future, at least in the wager that makes a future be present, not endlessly deferred. To think in terms of the future means to think as if anything is possible. But it is up to us to understand which of our possible futures will not make our future permanently impossible. I have often quoted Edward Said in this regard—"All criticism is postulated and performed on the assumption that it is to have a future"[6]—much as I have argued that Said's bequeathed lesson is for us to be at once skeptical and utopian. The presumed incompatibility between these two standpoints illustrates what I have been arguing here: The skeptic forces the utopian to be attentive to the present, to everything that passes before us in order to be judged; the utopian relieves the skeptic from the quicksand of self-absorption

6. See Edward Said, "The Future of Criticism," in *Reflections on Exile* (Cambridge, Mass.: Harvard University Press, 2000), 171.

into the negative. This makes utopia entirely the work of the present (not the displaced projection to a deferred future, which is actually a gesture of nostalgia)[7] and skepticism the work of what cannot present itself with the certainty that it is not a mere phantasm.

Of course, there is nothing prudent about this way of thinking. In any case, prudence is irreparably tainted by Latin-Christian meaning, which is why it is an inappropriate translation of Aristotelian *phronēsis*. In fact, I would propose that this sort of affirmative skepticism is a productive way to rethink the notion of *phronēsis* beyond its restricted translation by latter-day ethical Aristotelianism. If *phronēsis* is considered the praxis of thinking on the edge of the given, of *thaumazein* (that is, exercising critical judgments without preconceived norms and injunctions in astonishment before the world), then it involves a great deal of risk, indeed, danger. All transcendentalist ethics—and in societies that include or are products of a monotheistic imaginary, transcendentalism pretty much covers the ethical range—exist because they cannot handle the risk of *phronēsis*, the risk of thinking and making (*poiein*) a decision in the absence of a priori external norms and guarantees.

In *Nicomachean Ethics*, Aristotle names *phronēsis* as the key capacity that enables one to opt for the temperament of ethical virtue (*aretē*). He names ethos as an optional temperament (*hexis proairetikē*), that is, not a way of being that comes naturally or is derived from conformity to custom or order, as the product of a contract or the execution of a command, but rather as a conscious decision (*phronēsis*). This makes *phronēsis* a sort of noncredal commitment that assures the integrity of one's decisions, as provisional as they are in a real world that is groundless and abyssal. But the history of societies suggests that the cosmological abyss emerges more formidably when

7 Said is explicit on this when he speaks of art as a mode of thinking in utopian cast, "if by utopian we mean worldly, possible, attainable, knowable," in *Musical Elaborations* (New York: Columbia University Press, 1991), 105.

people are likely to embrace the provisional. It is a cliché to point out that religion is the most archaic, most consistent, and arguably most effective way to encounter the abyss with the most pronounced sense of control and permanent foundation. So, of course, is science in contemporary so-called secular societies. However, in either case the abyssal terrain is not vanquished. No mindful person can say, for example, that if you imagine that you can fly—which you do in your mind and most definitely actualize in your dreams, your visions, or your prayers—you can leap out of a tenth-floor window without landing straight down on the pavement in broken pieces. This is an abyssal externality that cannot be denied—abyssal in the sense that it cannot be bounded or mastered. We can call this a natural substratum, a *physis* without foundation, which cannot be overcome but nonetheless does not determine, in any straightforward causal sense, the capacity of the human to imagine, to envision, to dream, or to pray. Human beings ultimately did invent ways of flying, and it is remarkable that they did precisely because there is nothing in nature that suggests that they were meant to. Indeed, those prosthetic devices, whatever they may be, that enable humans to fly are themselves indelible reminders of the cosmological abyss that can be conquered but cannot be overcome.

The cosmological abyss is a mere phrase, of course, an image produced in language in order to configure this groundless and in fact intrinsically meaningless playing field of living being. In this groundless and meaningless field there are no limits to human life, to the extent that life hinges on the exercise of the imagination, except for one limit that is insurmountable no matter what the imagination conjures, and that is death. This sends us back to the tragic. This contradiction between the limitlessness of living in the world and the insurmountable limit that ends this living is what the tragic imagination takes as the point of departure. The tragic imagination created a theatrical art to address the impossible question: What do you do with limitlessness while living when you know that an unavoidable limit will end your living? As a specific art form, the tragic imagination settled on the understanding that the more you embodied this sense of unavoidable and insurmountable final limit, the more alertness and accountability you were to gain, because the stakes of mere life were raised even higher to confront your limitlessness within that limit. That's the point of the famous second ode in Sophocles's *Antigone*. Of course, it's very difficult to live in limitlessness, even when you know that at some point it will end and you will be relieved of the trouble. So we create limits all the time. That's what society is, first and foremost: a limit. Therefore, the issue is not that we create limits, but that we think about what limits are, about the fact that we create them and not someone else. It is in the demand for the decision of self-limitation that human beings become politically accountable.

I understand that the invocation of tragic life I am performing here may raise all kinds of questions about one's capacity for commitment in the absence of all guarantees, or even charges of disingenuousness: How can you speak of the lack of norms or the lack of normative guarantees and then proceed in fact to take positions? This is a genuine and difficult question that entails a rather acrobatic way of encountering the world, a "metabolic restlessness," in Kirstie McClure's brilliant poetic phrase,[8] because when one makes decisions, one inevitably steps into a space of creating norms of some kind, which one then presumably follows if one is at all responsible and accountable to one's decision. In no way does this mean, however, that these norms are unassailable, and nowhere can it be socially justified that these norms be prescribed or imposed on another, that they enact a framework for normalization, by which we mean a precondition. They may be decisive for the person who steps into

8. This is the phrasing Kirstie McClure used to describe the position taken in this argument in her response to the presentation of this essay during the *boundary 2* meetings at UCLA on May 12, 2012. I'm ever grateful for many of her suggestions, which have been incorporated here throughout.

the realm of decision, and in that instance they do produce an idiomatic sort of normative structure—idiomatic only in the sense that it pertains to an individual's condition that meets the standards of recognition and feasibility of a collective coexistence. But if in fact one's context of decision or one's context of encountering the other—whereby encounter means also coexistence—is provisional, meaning that it remains always open to question and to change, then these norms are unable to achieve the sort of transcendental foundation that would permit them to exist outside the context of decision, outside the struggle among convictions, outside the point of encounter, and ultimately outside the real terms of coexistence.

This is to reiterate, rather simply, that all guarantees are artificial; they are created by human beings, presumably in the realm of the living and not in some ancestral lifeless suspension. Or, even if they have indeed come to exist via some ancestral tradition, they are subject to the permission of the living. This is Thomas Paine's great lesson in his response to Edmund Burke's repudiation of the French Revolution. To speak of living life without guarantees is not to say that guarantees are never put into effect, because no society can exist without them. But like norms, guarantees have to be understood to have been placed there by us and not by extraterrestrials, and therefore, they are provisional, just as human life on this planet is provisional. This means, in addition, that just because we have placed limits there does not mean that we are done, that we can go home and expect them to serve us automatically, because then we permit limits, norms, guarantees to form an elsewhere that authorizes them, a transcendental foundation. Contrary to what ethicists who have come to rely on transcendental guarantees argue, a provisional encounter with the enigma of our existence in the world—which, I repeat, in the last instance is but the state of mere existence as such—does not imply lack of commitment to principles or to action. But it does suggest that all commitments must be reexamined. Any commitment that

remains unexamined ceases to be a commitment; it becomes
obedience to a certain kind of pattern, faithful to preordained
rules. In fact, my commitment to the other, to my loved one, is
first of all a commitment to reexamination. It cannot be conducted as custom or by prescription because then it actually
betrays the other; it treats the loved one as inert and unchange-
able, as transcendental completeness and closure.

This is why I reiterate here my critique of the tendency,
exemplified by Charles Taylor's *A Secular Age* and reproduced
by many of his acolytes, to celebrate transcendence as resistance to closure. The presupposition that the transcendent is
defined as what provides an opening is indefensible in and of
itself. One could easily argue just as well that the transcendental horizon is the epitome of closure insofar as it is constituted by the requirement that the world (and the worldly) is
enclosed in whatever lies beyond it, in whatever transcends it.
This beyond becomes precisely what closes off the infinite
unfolding of the worldly. We can have all kinds of arguments
about the limits of immanence and transcendence, but we
cannot allow closure to be posited as the de facto opposition
to transcendence that thereby validates it. In the end, the
point is not to be against transcendence and in favor of
immanence, for immanence too may be codified as a self-
enclosed and thus indisputable domain. This would make
immanence a transcendental domain too, in the precise sense
in which Andreas Kalyvas once argued that the transcendental simply signifies whatever domain is taken out of the field
of contestation.

Atheism is an existential position directed against both religious faith and transcendental reason equally, and it is based
on a tragic view of life, against which both morality and rationality (as unacknowledged derivatives of transcendentalism)
are driven. But atheism is also a historical horizon, a specific
social-imaginary signification, instituted at the same time
as theism, this religious imaginary in which divinity is an all-
consuming but singular, all-signifying but figureless, figure.

For atheism to vanish, all theism must vanish—as of now, an unimagined social-imaginary horizon. Perhaps such a horizon could be thought to bear the most credible meaning of the post-secular, but by then we will have done well to have invented another name.

FOUR

Confronting Heteronomy

To presume to speak under such a heading with an impetus to engage the real world is a bit of a folly, for confronting heteronomy is an almost impossible task beyond mere discourse. But it is something that Cornelius Castoriadis—whose thought I examine here in this light—spent his entire life thinking about and acting on, something that most people in most societies in the history of the world have surely avoided. So, despite the folly, the title stands, for it encapsulates the first and necessary step in all action that can be called, substantially, emancipatory action, which is what the project of autonomy foremost demands. This is all the more intriguing now that contemporary conditions have brought the question of emancipatory action to the forefront in overt political ways and from social-historical sources that would have been previously unfathomable (for example, what has been named, in rather cavalier fashion, the "Arab Spring").

I address these contemporary conditions elsewhere in detail, but I invoke them here because they do provide the social-historical impetus for what is otherwise a primarily philosophical inquiry. My idea is to stage a juxtaposition of two prominent domains in Castoriadis's thinking that have not otherwise been considered in tandem, especially when the project of autonomy is at the forefront of the inquiry, where usually (for understandable reasons) a thinker's likely tendency is to take an overtly political orientation. The two domains are Castoriadis's concern with the problem of the living being (*le vivant*) and his attempt to reconsider the epistemological terms within which we think, not merely the philosophical problems of existence (for him ontological and anthropological), but a kind of contemporary cosmology that engages the problem of chaos in the world we live in. Both can be thought of as natural-existential domains because they both engage with the problem of *physis*, but insofar as this is crossed by *nomos*, both are considerations of the enigma of the institution of society, that is, the mode by which human beings organize their natural-existential dimensions of living into a historical cosmos that becomes a source of meaning. Castoriadis never ceases to remind us of this. There is a third dimension essential to this particular configuration—the psychoanalytic dimension—about which I have spoken extensively however, so I skip it here, although it necessarily shadows the entire discussion.[1]

It is certainly worth noting in passing that a broad range of language emerging from Castoriadis's thought, especially about democracy and autonomy against barbarism, is nowadays surfacing explicitly in radical youth circles in many parts of the world, even outside Europe. This is implicated, of course, in the new radical democracy movements, which are taking place under a variety of names but share an impetus for political action outside established parameters of parliamentary

---

1. See "Philosophy and Sublimation," *Thesis Eleven* 49 (May 1997): 31–44; and "On Self-Alteration," *Parrhesia* 9 (Spring 2010): 1–17, http://www.parrhesia journal.org/.

liberalism without, however, basing themselves on the reproduction of clichés of revolutionary violence. It is this curious conjuncture that makes our reflections here ever more
urgent.

The most elemental understanding of Castoriadis's thinking
in relation to heteronomy is that heteronomy is self-instituted.
This simple realization is often overlooked, even though Castoriadis spoke almost from the outset of society's significational
closure precipitated by its self-occultation, except for rare
social-historical occasions where closure is partially broken.
Moreover, he always insisted on lucidity (which is not simply
self-consciousness in the traditional sense) whenever he attempted to configure the actions of social autonomy in various
ways over the years.

To say that heteronomy is self-instituted means that confronting heteronomy is nothing less than confronting oneself—
and, more precisely, one's own self-creation of an other who
stands in for one's self. There are all kinds of essential psychoanalytic dimensions to this, which, as I mentioned, I have addressed elsewhere, especially in relation to Castoriadis's notion
of self-alteration. I would add only that in the same way we
would argue that self-alteration is an essential conceptual component of the project of autonomy, repression of self-alteration
and the displacement of one's own alterity onto an external
figure are the essential components of heteronomy.

This displacement suggests that a heteronomous relation
operates in a double way. On the one hand, it necessitates the
internalization of various certainties or givens—or rather, more
accurately, of certain values, ideas, or practices that are internalized as given, indisputable, and unquestionable or, further
yet, become given, indisputable, and unquestionable by virtue
of being internalized and thus naturalized. Theodor Adorno
was especially keen on how "second nature" was the key trope
of socialization, of internalizing social institutions that, according to his metaphor, formed a kind of geological sedimen-

tation in the organization of subjectivity.[2] On the other hand, there is a certain kind of external heteronomy, that is, the compulsion or subjugation exercised on us by institutional power, whether it is corporeal or psychological, overt or tacit. No doubt, as necessary as the distinction is, the line between what is internalized and what is external heteronomy is always blurred, since no external heteronomy can ever be totally achieved without some last instance of internalization; hence the imperative of ideology. Consumerism, for example, epitomizes this blurring, reversing even people's internalized condition by their consent to an externally driven compulsion. The relentless desire for novelty in consumer addiction is predicated not on the desire to compete for commodities in society, to outshine the neighbors in fancy gadgets or performance of lifestyle, but on investment in ever renewing one's own phantasms, which then "suddenly" appear to be commensurate with what "objectively" exists as a trend. In today's waste capitalism, the creation of phantasms is hijacked from the individual's psyche and reproduced as external imposition.

Because heteronomy is a social condition that human beings institute for themselves, whatever counts as external here cannot belong to the realm of nature. The law of gravity makes it certain that if I jump off a building, I will crash and be shattered, and it is ridiculous to argue that for this reason it is an oppressive law because it does not allow me to fly. Parachutes or bungee cords, gliders or airplanes are glorious prosthetic inventions to defy the effect of this law, and they may even satisfy my crazy desire to fly, but obviously do not abolish the law

2. Adorno began configuring this argument through his concept of "natural history" in 1932, and it informs the entire range of his work, including his musical theory. The figure of sedimentation becomes especially apropos in relation to my later discussion of the figure of magma in Castoriadis. See, indicatively, Theodor Adorno, *Negative Dialectics*, trans. E. B. Ashton (New York: Seabury Press, 1973), 300–60.

that doesn't actually allow me to fly. We cannot possibly consider our subjection to the law of gravity an instance of heteronomy, even if gravity's alterity is indisputable and out-maneuverable. The alterity of the reality principle as such, whose culmination is death itself, cannot possibly be considered a source of heteronomy: "However we consider the matter, we cannot support the argument that death, or reality more gener-ally, are sources of heteronomy, precisely in the same way that we cannot conceive the existence of other individuals or of so-ciety as a source of heteronomy. Only collective existence exists; only social existence exists. It's ridiculous to think that 'hell is the others.' [The reference is to the famous line in Jean-Paul Sartre's *No Exit*.] The others may be a source of obstruc-tion, as may be reality itself, but they are equally a source of potential. Which it is of the two will always depend on what I am."[3] Heteronomy occurs not because law (*nomos*) belongs to an other (*heteron*), but because I make law into an other (in the full *poiētic* sense of making), because I have conferred on law an otherness that comes to seem intrinsic to it or, even more, to be a source of it.

———

I concur with Suzi Adams's analysis of a certain shift in Casto-riadis's trajectory of thinking about questions of *physis*, which perhaps can be configured as a turn of emphasis toward the study of the living being as such after having studied social-historical being, without meaning to suggest that the second is ever abandoned or overcome.[4] To be sure, Castoriadis's over-arching anthropological interest is evident even in the late *So-cialisme ou Barbarie* texts—it is as a result of this specific exigency that we might account for his turn toward psychoanalysis—but

3. See Cornelius Castoriadis, *Thucydide, la force et le droit* (Paris: Seuil, 2011), 93–94, and on heteronomy in general, 92–96.

4. Suzi Adams, *Castoriadis's Ontology: Being and Creation* (New York: Fordham University Press, 2011).

the turn to the consideration of living being specifically partakes of two trajectories of exploration starting in the early 1980s, the combination of which is precisely what concerns me here: (1) the examination of the ancient Greek imaginary as a particular cosmological proposition, especially as it was configured in the earliest social-historical manifestations of the *polis* even before democracy was instituted (hence the attention to pre-Socratic thinking), and (2) as part of Castoriadis's ongoing conversation with the sciences (both physics and mathematics, but also cognitive science), a sharper focus on ontological questions, and the elaboration of his understanding of *pour soi*, which has both psychoanalytic and biological dimensions, as well as an intrinsic connection to how the creative imagination eludes mathematization.

From his short comments on Francisco Varela's *Principles of Biological Autonomy* in the first issue of *Le Débat* in 1980, we know how much Castoriadis welcomed Varela's (and by extension Humberto Maturana's) groundbreaking contribution to the life sciences, which he saw as rigorously philosophical, not only because Varela and Maturana's thinking inaugurates a way of looking at the autonomy of the living being with a term that would have special resonance for Castoriadis (*autopoiesis*), but also because the image of the living organism sketched out from their *Autopoiesis and Cognition* (1972) onward dismantles the classic model of information science that assumes an organism to enact a cognitive mapping of already-formed external data that it receives as input from an objectively constituted nature. The dismantling of this model is achieved by reconfiguring entirely not only the previous model of the cognitive field as an already-constituted domain of coded information but also the very terms that have enabled this field to be thought as such.

Instead of asking, "How does an organism obtain information about its environment?" Varela and Maturana ask, "How does it happen that the organism has the structure that permits it to operate adequately in the medium in which it exists?"[5] In other words, the two biologists do not seek to interpret a passive condition of decoding but to determine the interactive domain that enables the categories "self/other" or "self/nonself" even to emerge and be signified. Thus they not only precipitate a shift from a semantic to a structural question but, moreover, identify the structural framework as predicated on a set of principles that are intricately and mutually determining in unconventional ways. Namely—and I summarize what is an exceedingly meticulous argument—they delineate a process (which is, however, not linear) according to the following steps:

1. Although every unity appears to work as a simple unity, it is in fact composite.
2. The recognition and transmission of whatever characterizes this unity (this organism) is readable in its components.
3. These components are not dictated by the objective pressures of the environment but are created by the organism itself according to its internal needs (autopoiesis).
4. These internally created components realize in turn the structure of the environment in which the organism exists.
5. The environment thus becomes a medium that enables this self-creation.
6. Living systems are thus (composite) units of self-creation and self-sufficiency that exist in an ambience of interplaying forms.

Although Maturana and Varela affirm the rather standard biological thesis that characterizes autonomous systems by their

5. Humberto Maturana and Francisco Varela, *Autopoiesis and Cognition: The Realization of the Living* (Boston: D. Reidel Publishing Company, 1980), xvi. Henceforth, page numbers are referenced in the text.

achievement of operational closure—in the algebraic sense of a system's operations remaining within the system's domain—they nonetheless reject models of closed systems, strictly non-interactive input/output systems. Operational closure for them consists in the basic sense of an organism's necessity to always have a precise sense of its limit, paradigmatically understood at the level of minimal cellular self-constitution but also reconstitution should this be necessary: "One of the most paradigmatic cases of operational closure is the very origin of life as the emergent unit of minimal cellular organization, where the biochemical closure of membrane constitution and metabolic repair make the cell a viable self-distinguishing autopoietic unit."[6] In other words, an organism's basic operational closure is necessary in order for interaction between organisms to be achievable at all and for environmental ambience to enable the autopoiesis of living beings, which, as we will see in a minute, will animate the differential process of alteration, of the emergence (indeed, Castoriadis would say creation) of *other* forms from within the ontic condition of the living being that ultimately exceed all figures of closure.

Along these lines of thinking, what makes *Autopoiesis and Cognition* a radical intervention is that unlike a typical biological treatise, it engages with the social environment of the human living being, and indeed with its politics. As autopoietic systems, the argument goes, human beings first and foremost engage in social operations that satisfy the terms of autopoiesis (according to what is desirable or undesirable for an organism's self-sustenance—not merely a physiological but a psychic process, which for Castoriadis would never be entirely separable), but such operations, insofar as they exist in an interactive medium, pertain directly to the overall social framework, which is characteristically described as a homeostatic balance (xxvii).

6. Francisco J. Varela and Paul Bourgine, eds., *Toward a Practice of Autonomous Systems* (Cambridge, Mass.: MIT Press, 1992), xii.

Although every social environment tends to sustain and reproduce itself (and is therefore conservative in the final instance),
Maturana and Varela argue that at times the autopoietic process of self-sustainment may produce components that the
social system will recognize as problematic. (Castoriadis would
add—to remember the psychoanalytic dimension—that it is
precisely at the point of developing a defunctionalized psy-
chism that human-being enables the rupture of the foundational cognitive closure of living being as such.) In response,
the system will either attempt to absorb the problematic components or will disengage itself from them, thereby enabling
the production of another system. This is indeed how Maturana
and Varela account for the alteration of living systems, and,
significantly from a Castoriadian standpoint, they characterize
the transformative (and thereby socially destabilizing) element
as "social creativity":

> This is why social creativity, as the generation of novel social rela-
> tions, always entails interactions operationally outside the society,
> and necessarily leads to the generation, by creative individuals, of
> modes of conduct that either change the defining relations of the
> society as a particular social system, or separate them from it. Social
> creativity is necessarily antisocial in the social domain in which it
> takes place. (xxvii–xxviii)

Social creativity brings forth an internal contradiction
within the system, which the system will in every instance attempt to restrict. For this reason, Maturana and Varela argue,
the organic inclination of societies is to be heteronomous. They
do not use the word, but this is in essence what they mean
when they speak of the tendency toward totalitarian organization that disallows the "observer positions"—that is, positions
that operate "as if external to the situation one finds oneself,
[which] allows him, if he has the proper experiences, to con-
template the societies that he integrates and to like them or
dislike them" (xxix). From the biological standpoint, if an autopoietic being finds the ambience undesirable, as it were, it will

seek to produce component modalities that will attempt to alter it, and either it will succeed or the structural coupling will fail and, as a dissident entity, it will be expelled in turn so as either to be extinguished or to help form other structures. Incidentally, Maturana and Varela also speak of those situations in human societies where the system "does not involve one's auto-poiesis as a constitutive feature of it" and thereby produces conditions of "social abuse." The institution of slavery, as the forceful incapacitation of autopoiesis in a specifically designated people, is an obvious example of such conditions.

They conclude with the following stipulation, which is amazing from the standpoint of typical biological thought:

> A human society in which to see all human beings as equivalent to oneself, and to love them, is operationally legitimate, without demanding from them a larger surrender of individuality and autonomy than the measure one is willing to accept for oneself while integrating it as an observer, is a product of human art, that is, an artificial society that admits change and accepts every human being as not dispensable. Such a society is necessarily a non-hierarchical society for which all relations of order are constitutively transitory and circumstantial to the creation of relations that continuously negate the institutionalization of human abuse. Such a society is in essence an anarchist society, a society made for and by observers that would not surrender their condition of observers as their only claim to social freedom and mutual respect. (xxix–xxx).

We do not need to get bogged down in specific words to understand that the sort of society described here is a democratic society of free and autonomous individuals and, in this respect, precisely anarchist insofar as the *archē* is marked, as Aristotle first argued in the *Politics*, by the autonomous sharing of both the *archon* and the *archomenos* position ("whereby the ruler learns by being ruled"). Even if the terms do not quite match, there is a lot of Castoriadis to recognize here, including the fact that the basic tendency of society is toward closure and assimilation of dissidence and that the breaking of this closure, the project of autonomy, is an abnormal development, a development against the grain, whose difficult art is the only desirable course of life for free human beings.

Let us recall that Castoriadis subscribed perfectly to the organizational closure of the living being in all cases as a necessary condition of self-determination that indeed also determines the knowledge of the boundaries between self and other—strictly speaking, self and nonself. "The living being [*le vivant*] cannot be but only by making be the distinction between self and non-self [*soi et non-soi*]. But this non-self cannot be for itself except by virtue of those modes determined by the self [*mais ce non-soi ne peut être pour lui que selon des modes determinés par le soi*]. As an immediate result, there is no sense in talking about 'representation' of the outside on the inside (or, in a terminology that is not Varela's own, it is the living being that creates the 'image' [of self]—both as *image* and as *such* an image [of self])."[7] But this dimension of strict organizational closure, as the very making of identity, is not to be understood, Castoriadis points out, strictly in the *ensidic* dimension.[8] Rather, it exceeds the self-regulating demands of calculating and organizing knowledge into self-enclosed and fully determined domains (in the likeness of mathematical sets) precisely because the material components of an organism's composite unity are self-created—and, one might say, re-created—as modes of knowledge and determination in the environmental space that marks the encounter between the organism and its world, be-

7. Cornelius Castoriadis, "Francisco Varela, *Principles of Biological Autonomy*" [review], *Le Débat* 1 (1980): 127.

8. *Ensidic* is a neologism that Castoriadis invented as shorthand for his notion of "ensemblist-identitary" thinking and developed extensively as early as *The Imaginary Institution of Society* (1975). ("Ensemble" in French is the mathematical term for set.) Ensidic logic is necessary to the existence of all living beings because it is the way in which each state of being identifies, organizes, calculates, and functionalizes its proper sphere of existence, including inevitably the sphere of existence of the other(s). The radical imagination of the human psyche, however, exceeds ensidic logic, operating in magmatic terms, as discussed later.

tween this being and that being, between being and Being, between self and other.

Let us also recall Castoriadis's insistence that between these encountering pairs, in their various registers, there does not exist a symmetrical correspondence, some sort of mirroring, precisely because, although these entities are radically self-sufficient, they are not inert, at the very least because they are not inanimate. They are living—which is also always to say, dying: that is, subjected to the order of time and therefore to alteration, to generation and degeneration. In other words, the encounter is always asymmetrical and dynamic, thereby opening the organism's components to new capacities of knowledge and comprehension of the world. In complex living systems and surely in human-being, this is implicated in the psychosocial construction of subjectivity and its interminable and unlimited phantasmatic capacity for creation of new forms. In their 1995 radio dialogue, Varela confirms that Castoriadis's understanding of an elemental phantasmatic *pour soi* that creates and organizes its own proper significational universe is commensurable with the biological findings about the autopoietic capacity of all living beings, which, as Varela says, precipitates an "imaginary excess" at a primary self-determining level that permeates the entire social sphere of determination.[9]

Castoriadis's response is to pinpoint in turn, from his perspective, one of the most inscrutable domains of knowledge: how this phantasmatic excess operates as somatic inscription. His attention to the corporeal aspect of the psyche is motivated, among other things, by his consistent critique of cybernetic or information-computation models of cognition, which are quintessential models of heteronomy. Without going here into the discussion of the affective *Vorstellung* of the human psyche and

9. Cornelius Castoriadis, *Postscript on Insignificance: Dialogues with Castoriadis* (London: Continuum, 2011), 61–62. See also Castoriadis, "Pour soi et subjectivité," in *Arguments pour une méthode: Autour d'Edgar Morin* (Paris: Seuil, 1990), 118–27.

thereby entirely into a psychoanalytic discussion, let us simply focus on the problem of the human capacity of thought (*phantasia* in Aristotelian terms) and specifically on the fact that no creative knowledge can be achieved without passion, which is not merely affect but somatic expression of the singular experience of human-being as a condition of life. For Castoriadis, experience is signified in a double register: on the one hand, through the French notion of *expérience* as an experimental encounter with one's world, and on the other hand, through the Greek notion of *peira* (and its relation to *peras*), which imbues the meaning of experience with an outmaneuverable condition of the limit of time, the fact of finitude and mortality. We have, in other words, a fabulous interweaving of signification (experiment and finitude) that does indeed make human experience incalculable, unformalizable, and unreproducible—in Castoriadis's term, magmatic. On this basis of configuring knowledge for the living being, Castoriadis and Varela concur that the creative (autopoietic) capacity of living being, of *pour soi*, exceeds all ensidic dimensions and opens up the specific terrain of cognition that will enable us to confront heteronomy as a problem of our own making and, therefore, as a condition that can be unmade, even if with enormous difficulty.

Confronting heteronomy is inevitably a political matter, but it demands a shift in social-imaginary institutions and thereby involves many other dimensions, not least an overcoming of traditional ontological and cosmological attitudes. An understanding of experience as substantially experimental and finite configures an understanding of living being as an essentially temporal mode implicated in the creation and destruction of forms. This means a poietic mode of being—not just autopoietic, poietic of self, but rather poietic of the other, or more precisely, autopoietic of the other. This mode of being creates alterity first as an inherent dimension of the self and second (not sequentially, but grammatically speaking) as a necessary dimension of the world. Hence Castoriadis's notion of *à-être* as a condition of both tending toward and intending being, being as continuously becoming being both by tendency and by intention. In other words, Being can never be fully constituted as a space of plenitude and identity even though every living being necessarily has a primordial sense of itself (primary signification) as an order of plenitude and identity with/in its proper world (*Eigenwelt*). As *à-être*, the ontological dimension bears an inherent alterity, much as it enacts the *poiētic* formation of alterity and self-alteration. Moreover, because cosmological time is precisely delineated by the creation/destruction of forms in a trajectory of alteration through time, being is a temporal notion as much as it is *poiētic*. From this standpoint, one might say that Castoriadis alters Varela's configuration by restoring the *physis/nomos* distinction (while, of course, retaining their necessary entwinement and tension), and this is how we might chart the shift from autopoiesis to autonomy.[10]

Castoriadis's ontological thinking partakes of a pre-Socratic cosmological language that posits an abyssal and infinite chaos as the generative pool of a cosmos that comes to be formed, by virtue of the ineluctable exigency of time, as a finite but ever-renewable world of meaning and being. Living being specifically is self-constituted in part by its irrepressible desire for meaning, for making (*poiein*) meaning. This desire for poietically making meaning, which in the ancient Greek world is expressed in the outmaneuverable social-historical institution of myth—without myth we cannot speak of a Greek social imaginary—emerges in the background of total meaninglessness, of non-sense, or in Castoriadis's language the *a-sensed*: "The Greek myths are true because they unveil a signification of the world that cannot be reduced to any kind of rationality, a signification that constantly presents a sense of things over a

---

10. See, indicatively, Suzi Adams, "Castoriadis and Autopoiesis," *Thesis Eleven* 88 (February 2007): 76–91.

background of the a-sensed [*les sens sur le fond de a-sensé*], a background of non-sense, whereby the non-sense is presented as everywhere penetrated by sense."[11] He adds that the singular importance of Greek myth is not that it reveals the signification of rationality; rather, "it unveils as ultimate signification of the world the lack of meaning [*a-sensé*] and that meaning emerges, as a figure, on the ground of this meaninglessness, while always being condemned, however, to return to this ground" (*CQFG*, 169).[12]

Quinstessential in this configuration of sense and non-sense, of meaning and meaninglessness, is the handful of words, known as the Anaximander fragment, that encapsulate the Greek social imaginary, particularly the broader horizon of understanding the permutations of *archē*, all the way to the institution of tragedy and, of course, democracy.[13] Anaximander is the first to give language to a notion of the infinite (*apeiron*), not in the sense in which it was later mathematized, but as the groundless, meaningless, and indeterminate space from which a determined, meaningful, and finite cosmos emerges—or rather is formed—and to which it returns. It returns because it

11. Cornelius Castoriadis, *Ce qui fait la Grèce: D'Homère à Héraclite* (Paris: Seuil, 2009), 167–68; henceforth cited in the text as *CQFG* followed by the page number.

12. The mythical and the mathematical can never overcome each other and are fully entwined in each other's terms: "There is no society without myth, and there is no society without arithmetic. And still more important, there is no myth (or poems or music) without arithmetic—and certainly, too, there is no arithmetic without myth (be it the myth of the 'pure rationality' of arithmetic)." Cornelius Castoriadis, "The Logic of Magmas and the Question of Autonomy," in *The Castoriadis Reader*, ed. David Ames Curtis (Oxford: Blackwell, 1997), 307. I discuss this text extensively later. All further passages are cited in the text as "LoM" followed by the page number.

13. I discuss the Anaximander fragment at length (including Castoriadis's analysis of it) in "*Archē*," *Political Concepts: A Critical Lexicon* 2 (Winter 2012), http://www.discoursenotebook.org/politicalconcepts/arche-stathis-gour gouris/; translated into Hebrew in *Mafteakh*, http://mafteakh.tau.ac.il.

must pay recompense—in decay, degeneration, death—for having disrupted the infinite fold. In this imaginary, not death but life itself constitutes an injustice, which is why this is a tragic imaginary, but also why it is an imaginary in which the question of justice is a cosmic (worldly) affair and never a matter of theodicy or any sort of transcendental categorical principle. The *chaos/cosmos* divide—which does not register a chasm but is rather an ever-conflicted relation—is echoed in a series of such dyadic antagonisms: *hubris/dike, physis/nomos, einai/ phainesthai*, and so on, which, in the Greek imaginary (at least until Plato) preclude the tendency toward a unitary ontology, thereby providing an interstitial opening for the radical interrogation necessary to the project of autonomy: "Unitary ontology, in whatever guise, is essentially heteronomous. The emergence of autonomy in Greece was conditioned by the nonunitary view of the world that is expressed from the beginning in Greek myths."[14] This nonunity is not configured in the struggle between the infinite and the finite, the indeterminate and the determined, as if they are two polarities as different universes. The struggle takes place within the infinite; what is determined to be (to live and to die) emerges determined within the interminable and indeterminable nonunitary to-be (*à-être*).

The paradoxical figure of the ontological injustice of death being at the same time a reconstitution of the order of the infinite and therefore a gesture of justice against the injustice of existence disrupting the infinite fold suggests a social imaginary that takes irrevocable death as the ultimate limit of living being, the only untranscendable limit that thereby frees life from any other imposed limits. (For "limits" we might also want to write "determinations.") It may seem, then, that heteronomy is removed from the realm of necessity in the course of one's

14. Cornelius Castoriadis, "The Greek Polis and the Creation of Democracy," in *Philosophy, Politics, Autonomy*, ed. David Ames Curtis (New York: Oxford University Press, 1991), 105.

life and relegated to one and only one place: death. But in death there is no *nomos*, strictly speaking. *Nomos* occurs and has meaning only in the course of living. So the untranscendable limit of death is not the last instance of a naturalized heteronomy but precisely the irrevocable limit point that denaturalizes heteronomy altogether. From this standpoint, limits or determinations in the course of one's life are open to becoming a matter of self-knowledge, self-determination, autonomy—in the strictest sense of determining the question of what is *nomos* within one's conditions of living. In his analysis of Anaximander, Castoriadis points out the *co-incidence* between Anaximander's fragment and the Aeschylean imagination in *Prometheus Bound*, specifically the notion of *physis* subject to (or crossed by) *nomos* and thereby opening the path for the creation of an autonomous life in a tragic universe (*CQFG*, 113). In this respect, tragedy itself, as a particular form of social and poetic practice, is exemplary of giving expression to the ontological chaos that permeates all existence and thus precipitates the conditions for human beings to realize that (1) there is a necessity for *nomos*, for otherwise life is defeated by its own meaninglessness; and (2) this necessity does not confine humans to a de facto subjugation to *nomos* because it opens the way for them to create meaning and the frameworks of meaning.

This path, the path of autonomy, is quintessentially *poiētic*. If the cosmos of all living being is characterized by a formative capacity to create itself, an elemental *vis formandi*, Castoriadis argues, then human-being is characterized in addition by a *libido formandi*: "To the potential for creation found in being in general, the human sphere adds a desire for formation. I call this potential and this desire the '*poietic*' element of humanity. Reason itself, in its specifically human form (which is not the same as the rationality intrinsic to animals, for example), is but an offspring." He goes on: "When man organizes rationally— ensidically—he does nothing but reproduce, repeat, or prolong already existing forms. But when he organizes poietically, he gives form to the Chaos."[15] Tragedy is one of the most glorious forms of this *poiētic* organization, for its very object, the crux of what it presents or performs, is the Chaos of Being itself. In a double gesture that, on the one hand, exemplifies the extraordinary capacity of the human imagination to create meaning in a poetic form that, on the other hand, presents the brutal reality of the ultimate incapacity of human beings to be masters over the meaninglessness of their existence resides the tragic character of autonomy.

Confronting heteronomy thus requires not only an acceptance of a tragic way of life but also a *poiētic* existence in response. What do I mean? If we think of Castoriadis's notion of chaos in relation to Anaximander's infinite *archē*, then human being itself, insofar as it cannot be reduced to a mere actualization/animation of organic matter but is characterized by its capacity for a lucid creation of societal institutions, is, in its short finite existence, a mode of giving form to the chaos from which it emerges. However, because the very existence of society's imaginary institution almost always tends toward the occlusion of chaos as such, any mode of giving form to chaos— not as reproduction of instituted forms but as creation of new forms—must be simultaneously a process of uncovering chaos (Castoriadis calls it *dévoilement*), of making chaos visible as the generative background on which human being's *poiētic* force is enacted. Castoriadis sees this uncovering as an interruption of the quotidian flow of already-established (instituted) forms, a tearing (*déchire*) of the apparently evident. Uncovering chaos and giving it form are one and the same thing, an extraordinary simultaneity that interrupts all established time flow.[16] In

---

15. Cornelius Castoriadis, "Culture in a Democratic Society," in *The Castoriadis Reader*, 342–43.

16. Cornelius Castoriadis, *Fenêtre sur le Chaos* (Paris: Seuil, 2007), 134–35.

the language we have been engaging so far, this tearing is the point where *nomos* intersects with *physis*. In the sense that this uncovering/forming is the moment of *poiēsis* (a "lucid drunkenness," Castoriadis calls it in an inspired phrase), then autonomy is quintessentially *poiētic*. And although Castoriadis never says so directly, I would argue that the *poiētic* process that is intrinsic to the project of autonomy—a project that is interminable insofar as there is no *telos* of it that remains uninterrogated—is a kind of permanently open window onto Chaos.

———

This *poiētic* existence, this openness to chaos, cannot be explained. At least, it cannot be explained in the sense that it can be fully accounted for, that it can be fully analyzed and categorized, although inevitably the fact that we use language at all even to describe it partakes of this domain of explicability or analyzability. Questions then arise about its epistemology. If we cannot quite know it, then what mode of knowledge does it enact? What is its relation to plain analytic knowledge or calculation? How can we even describe (since we cannot quite explain or account for) its cognitive capacity? Motivated by this same problem of describing *poiētic* existence and the same questions about how poetic cognition exceeds analytic knowledge, I argue in *Does Literature Think?* that the cognitive capacity of literature, as opposed to philosophy, is mythographic and performative. Here I am interested in what Castoriadis has described as a magmatic mode of knowledge as opposed to the totalizing explanation of mathematical knowledge because, in the last instance, confronting heteronomy demands a praxis that is not adequately conducted by the cunning of reason or the skills of calculation.

Castoriadis's earliest definition of magma as a mode of organization (of knowledge or of being) was construed specifically to counter the mathematical notion of a set (in French, *ensemble*): "A magma is that from which one can extract (or in which one can construct) an indefinite number of ensemblist organizations but which can never be reconstituted (ideally) by a (finite or infinite) ensemblist composition of these organizations."[17] A later statement, arising out of a discussion of magma in relation to the psyche, is less directly mathematical: "A magma's mode of being signifies simply that the object under consideration is neither reducible to these *ensidic* organizations nor exhaustible by them."[18] In both accounts, the magma and the set (ensemble) are not situated in simple opposition or difference. A magma exceeds the set in the sense that, as the first definition has it, it can include a set or a set may be extracted from it but, on the one hand, it cannot be reconstituted on the basis of this extracted or constructed set and, on the other hand, as the second definition clarifies, it can neither be reduced to a set nor exhausted by it. A simple way to think of this relation is to say that although magmas can generate sets, sets cannot (de)generate into magmas. In other words, what Castoriadis signified as ensidic logic cannot adapt itself to or entail a magmatic mode of being without utterly dissipating, while from a magmatic pool of determinations, an ensidic organization may emerge or be constructed. "Ideally, starting from magmas, we should try to describe ensembles as 'immersed in' magmas" ("LoM," 296), but no magma "can be partitioned into magmas" ("LoM," 297), in the sense that all notions of partition or categorization (as opposed to immersion) are possible only within ensidic logic. A magma is never totalizable, which is to say simultaneously that it is neither ever fully determined nor ever exhaustible; hence "every decomposition of magmas into ensembles leaves a magma as residue" ("LoM," 297). This inexhaustibility of the magmatic mode sustains the possibility of potentially interminable generation not only of ensembles (sets) but also of ruptures, creations, or altogether new determinations— radically new precisely in the sense that they are nonderivative

17. Cornelius Castoriadis, *The Imaginary Institution of Society*, trans. Kathleen Blamey (Cambridge, Mass.: MIT Press, 1987), 343.

18. Cornelius Castoriadis, "Done and to Be Done," in *The Castoriadis Reader*, 379.

of whatever is in place, because derivation too (like categorization or partition) is possible only within ensidic logic.

There are two issues that concern us in this context before I return to the question of autonomy and heteronomy proper: the question of determinacy and the question of the radically new. The main reason that drove Castoriadis to invent the notion of magma was the need to account for domains of being that cannot be fully determined or fully categorized, but without ceding ground to some sort of unqualified skepticism or radical contingency, which he always argued were in any case nonsensical positions in a physical universe of mathematical laws. One of the key domains that defy this universe while existing fully within it—whose elucidation provided, in fact, the initiative for the formulation of magma—is the radical imagination, which for Castoriadis ultimately consists of the human animal's capacity to conceive things that have never previously existed in any way, shape or form. Hence the question of radical creation is intimately linked to the question of determinacy, of what is indeterminate in ensidic terms but determinate and determining in a magmatic sense.

Much has been made in negative critiques of the notion of creation ex nihilo, one of Castoriadis's most controversial philosophical tropes. Given what we have rehearsed so far, we do not really need to wonder why Castoriadis insists on this figure. His entire anthropo-ontological framework is based on the idea that what distinguishes the human animal specifically is the capacity to create form (*eidos*) that is entirely unprecedented, previously inconceivable, and indeed nonexistent in any sense prior to the moment and fact of its creation. He insists time and again that creation does not entail the production of difference but the emergence of otherness. This capacity for the wholly new, the wholly other, is what distinguishes the radical imagination. The ex nihilo is there to accentuate the fact that we are not talking about reformulation, infinite variation, creative assembly, or rearrangement of already-existing forms. His example that the invention of the wheel is a more radical and splendorous creation in the universe than a new galaxy is well known, for every new galaxy emerging in space is ultimately but another instance of the galaxy form, whereas the wheel was entirely unprecedented.[19] The often used idiomatic injunction in English encapsulates what Castoriadis has in mind: "You're reinventing the wheel!" means that you are not being creative, you are not using your imagination, you are wasting your effort in reproducing what exists (however we are to consider the merits or inevitabilities of this kind of effort).

But Castoriadis—especially in late years and in order to defend himself from likely misunderstandings—insisted on the clarification that ex nihilo did not mean *in nihilo* or *cum nihilo*. Unprecedented radical creation out of nothing does not mean with(in) nothing, in a vacuum. On the contrary, what makes it radical is precisely that it takes place in history, *as* history— that indeed, it makes history anew. There is no way such creation can register as history anew without destroying, in some form or other, what exists in place, whether we conceive this as simply what resists the new or merely what resides there unwitting of whatever will newly emerge to displace it or efface it. New social-imaginary creations do contribute to the vanishing of social-imaginary institutions already there. That's why we don't have Pharaonic priests, Spartan warriors, or Knights of the Round Table running around in the streets of New York or the suburbs of Paris.

In retrospect, it is possible to construct a description—to write a history—of how and what elements and processes characterize the creation of new social-historical being. A common

19. "The wheel revolving around an axis is an absolute ontological creation. It is a greater creation, it weighs, ontologically, more than a new galaxy that would arise tomorrow evening out of nothing between the Milky Way and the Andromeda. For *there are already* millions of galaxies—but the person who invented the wheel, or a written sign, was imitating and repeating *nothing* at all." Castoriadis, *Imaginary Institution of Society*, 197.

example in Castoriadis, discussed at various junctures in his
work and arguably culminating in the years that made up the
seminars of *Ce qui fait la Grèce* (1982–85) is how the specifics of
the reforms of Cleisthenes that encapsulate the creation of Athenian democracy as a new social-historical being are "traceable"—if
that is the proper word—to the complexities of the social-
imaginary institution of the Greek *polis*, which Castoriadis
duly follows all the way back to the earliest Greek textual
documentation—Homer, Hesiod, Anaximander, Sappho. In
this sense, Castoriadis's theory of creation ex nihilo may not be
entirely unrelated to various theories of discontinuity in history. I cannot pursue this line of comparison here, but it is a
worthwhile path of reflection to consider the line, otherwise
alien to Castoriadis, that extends (in the French tradition, at
least) from Bachelard to Foucault. If we do not adhere dog-
matically to the notion of the "epistemological rupture" characteristic of this line—in the same way in which we would not
heed the accusations against Castoriadis that creation ex nihilo
ushers some sort of theology in the back door—then we might
arrive at a more nuanced understanding of the notion.[20]

But there is another dimension to this issue that I think
has not been adequately attended to. In his classic essay "Fait
et à faire" (1989), Castoriadis speaks of what grants validity to
creation—its encounter with the world. I quote extensively:

> Newton certainly did not "discover," he invented and created the
> theory of gravitation; but it happens (and this is the why we are still
> talking about it) that this creation *encounters* [*rencontre*] in a fruit-
> ful way *what is*, in one of its strata.
>
>   We create knowledge. In certain cases (mathematics) we also
> create, thereby, the *outside time*. In other cases (mathematical phys-
> ics) we create under the constraint of encounter; it is this encounter
> that validates or invalidates our creations.

20. See Laurent Van Eynde, "Castoriadis et Bachelard: Un imaginaire en
partage," *Cahiers critiques de philosophie* 6 (Summer 2008): 159–78.

And later:

> To the extent that we can effectively comprehend something about
> a foreign society, or say something valid about it, we proceed to
> a re-creation of significations, which encounter the originary cre-
> ation. . . . A being without the re-creative capacity of the imagina-
> tion will understand nothing about it.[21]

Let us focus for a moment on two elements: "the constraint
of encounter" and "the re-creative capacity of the imagination." The first is precisely to emphasize that ex nihilo does not
mean *in nihilo* or *cum nihilo*. Not only is radical creation out of
nothing always enacted in the world, but it is enacted as and
constrained by an encounter. The "nothing" out of which radical creation emerges exists, in the most precise sense, in the
world; it is not, in other words, some sort of transcendental
nowhere. And although we should not at all compromise the
notion—we indeed mean out of nothing; we mean, in the
ancient Greek sense, to note the passage "out of nonbeing into
being"—we have to allow ourselves the paradoxical capacity to
imagine both that this nothing, this nonbeing, is worldly and
that, instantly upon coming to be something, this newly created being registers its worldliness by an unavoidable encounter
with what exists, whether in the ensidic dimension of logic and
calculation or beyond it, in the *poiētic* dimension as such.

There is, in other words, a dimension of determination in
ex nihilo creation because any radical imaginary creation
always posits something—the new—in relation to something
else—what is. But by bringing into being something not in
connection with (not previously determined by) something
that is, one thereby alters the terms of relation of "what is"
or otherwise creates terms of relation that did not previously
exist: "The imaginary institution of society boils down to the
constitution of 'arbitrary' points of view, starting from which

---

21. Castoriadis, "Done and to Be Done," 396–97.

'equivalences' and 'relations' are established" ("LoM," 305). The words in quotation marks in this statement are what ensidic logic identifies as necessary to situations of complexity and multiplicity. But what is "necessary" or intrinsic to the process is the magmatic "arbitrariness" of complexity or multiplicity— even if "arbitrariness" too is ensidic wording. Determination and organization of material cannot possibly happen if this material does not have an intrinsic capacity to be organized and determined, "if the 'material' does not already include in itself the 'minimal form' of being formable" ("LoM," 306). In this sense, we come back to what Maturana and Varela found to be an essential dimension of living systems against the precepts of information science or cybernetic knowledge, namely, that an organism must already possess a structure (in their language) that permits it to operate within the medium in which it exists, an inherent capacity to form itself in its environment, so that the environment does not dictate its formation.

The ensidic dimension of the environment, of course, exists everywhere; without it, we cannot even ask the question "What is?" Yet, however we are to conceive and ask the question, "what is is not fully determined. What is is Chaos with irregular stratification" ("LoM," 307)—quite literally, a magma. No one would feel the need to underline that a magma exists if we were talking about volcanoes, just as no one would feel the need to account for the fact that what a volcanic magma "contains" cannot ultimately be differentiated—fully determined—in the various singular terms. The aspects of what makes a magma cannot be separately determined. Magmas are characterized precisely by this nondetermination, which is hardly to say that they are of indeterminate existence, unknown, inconceivable. "The nondetermination of what is is not mere 'indetermination' in the privative and ultimately trivial sense. It is creation, namely, emergence of *other* determinations, new laws, new domains of lawfulness. . . . No state of being is such that it renders impossible the emergence of determinations *other* than those already existing" ("LoM," 308).

The emergence of this otherness from within what already exists, and not because otherness exists in abstract transcendental fashion in some nonplace of being other, is what autonomy is all about. Autonomy implies *auto-heterōsis*, to use Castoriadis's Greek term for self-alteration. Contrary to both Kantian derivations and information science models of self-sufficiency, self-constitution, and self-referentiality, Castoriadis argues with exceptional clarity:

> Autonomy is not closure but, rather, opening: ontological opening, the possibility of going beyond the informational, cognitive, and organizational closure characteristic of self-instituting, but *heteronomous* beings. It is ontological opening, since to go beyond this closure signifies altering the already existing cognitive and organizational "system," *therefore* constituting one's world and one's self according to *other* laws, *therefore* creating a new ontological *eidos*, another self in another world. ("LoM," 310; italics in the original)

In this sense, autonomy—which, let us recall, is always social autonomy, not some sort of individual state—is a state of incompleteness, much like, for Anaximander, the infinite (*apeiron*) is literally, as the word has it, incomplete. For this elementary reason, autonomous being has absolutely nothing to do with models of autotelic or automatic being, contrary to what is often bizarrely argued. Even if we were to assume, as we would have to, that the *telos* of autonomous being would be to sustain itself, this *telos* can hardly be the mere extension or repetition of a status quo. This *telos* would have to undergo its continuous othering, the making (*poiein*) of "another self in another world," as Castoriadis says, for every configuration of purpose or end would have to be subjected to inquiry and evaluation anew, for no *nomos* of ends and purposes can emerge or be fashioned to exist outside the "self"—the *auto*—that decides and institutes.

This is why autonomy cannot be relegated to simple self-constitution—to recall here Castoriadis's sole critique of Maturana and Varela. First, all being, regardless of qualification, is always self-constituted, whether we think of this in terms of organic matter or atomic particles or societies and cultures. An autonomous community—say, in modern historical terms, the Kronstadt Commune or the anarcho-syndicalist councils in Barcelona—is characterized by having made self-constitution an explicit and articulate process that demands and achieves specific political institutions. This process is not a matter of mere uncovering, of rolling back the occlusion, because once self-constitution is elucidated with regard to what it is, its terrain is formally altered. It ceases to be an automatic process, always counted on to work in the same way, whether naturalized, theologized, or technologized, and becomes a framework of creative inquiry and formation, a *poiëtic* framework, which enables the chaos that never ceases to underlie it to emerge. This is why autonomy also cannot be adequately understood as sovereignty, as mastery of power. A self-organized, self-governing community—a democracy in the uncompromising sense of the term—is constituted on the basis of always questioning and examining the process of decision, which is in the last instance necessarily collective, even if it is made by a specific delegate or statesman (in the ancient sense), because no individual is sovereign separate from the community. Sovereignty is always lurking within democracy, but the *kratos* of the *demos* can never exist, not just practically but even conceptually, without the *demos*. Popular sovereignty, or, if you will, the people's mastery of power, is surely an inadequate term to describe a *kratos* that is always in the making by a *demos* always in the making (and most definitely unmaking, as the story of democratic Athens demonstrates), that is, a continuous process open to *poiësis*.[22]

This opening to *poiësis* is also an opening to knowledge—self-knowledge, of course, which is to say, in the terms discussed here, self-knowledge of the otherness inherent in the

---

22. "Mastery is an illusion. If we hold onto the idea of mastery we end up with the good society as it was defined once and for all by a philosopher—that is, we end up in heteronomy." Castoriadis, *Fenêtre sur le Chaos*, 67.

self, of the self's capacity for othering. This knowledge too is *poiētic*; that is, it is not exhausted in analytic (ensidic) understanding. Even more, in exceeding the ensidic dimension, this mode of knowledge mobilizes a sort of understanding that recognizes the necessity, even if inadequacy, of the ensidic. To the contrary, any form of being that inhabits fully ensidic parameters is impervious to this knowledge. Being immersed in a heteronomous condition means that one cannot know this heteronomy—this is elementary. Whatever one would know in such a condition—and it can be described and understood in profound detail: legal institutions, political states, sacred practices, and givens of all kinds—one could never know it as heteronomy, at least, not without creating other conditions to overcome it, which would be in itself an act of autonomy.

In this respect, all politics in the tradition of so-called self-organization or self-government is adequate to its name only insofar as its modes of action explicitly target the problem of heteronomy. It's easy to say, of course, but inordinately difficult to conduct because the very institution of society derives its meaning (and certainly produces meaning) from occluding the chaotic and groundless meaninglessness that underlies our existence, the organization (or *nomos*) of which it confers on authorities that transcend society and institutions. This curious and contradictory simultaneity of occluding the very thing that you organize and signify (give meaning to) is the immense power of society's institution. This is why it is nearly impossible, why it seems like folly, to resist. "The system holds together because it succeeds in creating people's adherence to the way things are."[23] So the point is not only to change the way things are, to imagine and create things otherwise, but to understand and elucidate the ways and means by which this adherence is created. And here, we return to the double process by which

---

23. Cornelius Castoriadis, "From Ecology to Autonomy," in *The Castoriadis Reader*, 241.

heteronomy works. For such profound adherence to "what is" cannot be actualized by sheer imposition. It requires an internalized motivation, a kind of performance of will (in fact, desire) over something that is too glorious to resist, not just because it inspires awe or even fear, but because it induces pleasure, and indeed, at times, the pleasure of being absorbed in the making of its glory.

Such is the provenance of the sacred—not merely what has come to be called religion, but anything that achieves sacred status in a particular society and culture. Such things would certainly include, in today's so-called secular societies, the seduction of technoscience and rational mastery, the "right" to economic prosperity, the fetish of modernity, the (pseudo)ideal of progress and development, etc., but equally, the (pseudo) ideal of ancestry and tradition, the fetish of the nation, the sacrosanctity of the Constitution and any other institution of law that makes Law into an ideal. To these, we could add, of course, all kinds of other transcendentalisms, of both ethics and aesthetics, and surely of politics, where politics—often, alas, in the very name of democracy—is utterly theological. In Castoriadis's language: "The sacred is the instituted simulacrum of the Abyss: religion confers a figure or figuration upon the Abyss and this figure is presented as both Ultimate Meaning and source of all meaning" ("LoM," 315). We would not want to restrict this just to religion, of course—and Castoriadis himself has spoken of the allure of technoscience in exactly the same terms—but the point is accurate nonetheless. Indeed, religion—or what we have come to identify as religion—does operate both as end and as source of all meaning, thereby emptying out the signifying field and paralyzing people's radical capacity to imagine and create wholly other meanings or even, more simply, the capacity to recognize and encounter the cosmic meaninglessness as is for what it is.

This is not just to point again to a tragic predicament. Encountering the cunning of the sacred is more than just unveiling or repealing the occultation of the underlying chaos because the cunning of the sacred consists not only in occulting chaos but simultaneously in presenting chaos and giving it form. It is this simultaneity, this duplicity, that desacralization aims to break. For there is nothing to be unveiled. Or, if you will, veiling forms the Nothing, and this would be fine if it did not disavow this nothingness, this meaninglessness, if the occulting act of the sacred did not obliterate "the *metacontingency* of meaning, namely the fact that meaning is a creation of society, that it is radically contingent for anyone who stands on the outside, and absolutely necessary for those who stand on the inside—therefore, neither necessary nor contingent" ("LoM," 315–16). This obliteration holds equally for the religiously devout and for the rationalist-secularist or the cultural nationalist—whenever socially instituted phantasms are worshiped as *what is* above all.

Confronting heteronomy, then, comes down to desacralizing *nomos*, to recognizing that there can never be any law that exists because it must, because it is necessary, or that there can never be any law that exists in the name of something other than it, in its social-historical particulars, not only God, but the Nation, the Ancestors, the Father, the People, or any Right or Reason, any Constitution or Legislator, and so on—any Law— that exists in some transcendental categorical Elsewhere.

FIVE

The Void Occupied Unconcealed

Claude Lefort's contribution to political theory, especially theories of bureaucracy and totalitarianism, modernity, and democracy, is enormous. Yet much of Anglophone scholarship in recent years has been drawn primarily to "The Permanence of the Theologico-Political?" (1981), an essay read largely in isolation from the complexity of an oeuvre that spans more than fifty years. This tendency is symptomatic. This particular essay has commanded such attention because it has been absorbed into the wildly proliferating discussion of political theology and secularism. Yet the "theologico-political" in Lefort has as much to do with the current framework of political theology in the American academy as Carl Schmitt's famous *Political Theology* (1923) had to do with Spinoza's *Theologico-Political Treatise* (1670). Obviously, the compound "theologico-political" should not be assumed to slide unquestionably into the reverse "political theology." Spinoza is historically the first to use the hyphenated adjectival substantive, while the noun that now almost claims to be an epistemological topos has an ancient history in the trajectory of Christianity.[1] However, both names, regardless of how they are compounded, can no longer be assumed to evade the signification of modernity. Their trajectory in Western (essentially Christian) thought has moved from the initial tension between realms of the sacred (theological) and the profane (political) to an association between them that leaves no bounds for interpretation privileging one term over another according to specific historical needs.

Although nothing can be discounted in the coincidence of names, all names are historically bound to matters beyond their naming, which at the very least raises questions about the mere association of concepts on the basis of their name. To what extent, if any, Lefort's essay is to contribute to current discourses of political theology or secularism is open to question and worthy of inquiry. My examination of it here is conducted in the broader context of examining the problem of heteronomy within the imaginary of modernity. Whatever significance the essay may have for the problematic of secular criticism is to be sought precisely in the way it exemplifies Lefort's twofold contemplation of, on the one hand, the question of society's historical genesis and, on the other hand, society's democratic actualization. Restoring the broader framework of how this essay works in the milieu of Lefort's thinking may

---

1. For an exhaustive account of the trajectory of political theology as a concept, see Annika Thiem, "Political Theology," in *The Encyclopedia of Political Thought*, ed. Michael Gibbons (Oxford: Blackwell, 2012). For an informative contextualization of Lefort's essay in the political-theological discussion in contemporary French thought, see Paul Valadier, "Permanence du théologico-politique politique et religion, de nouvelles donnes," *Recherches de Science Religieuse* 94 (April 2006): 547–70; and Warren Breckman, "Democracy between Disenchantment and Political Theology: French Post-Marxism and the Return of Religion," *New German Critique* 94 (Winter 2004): 72–105. Breckman's historical scholarship is impeccable, but his stipulation of a "return to religion" is overstated even if it is meant as simple rhetoric.

perhaps help disengage it from easy and expedient interpretations in fashionable discourses.

Lefort's consistent impetus was to elucidate the generative
instances in the institution of society, which for him were tantamount to the various situations of the emergence of the political. Like that of Cornelius Castoriadis, his fellow interlocutor
and founder of *Socialisme ou Barbarie* (1948–65), Lefort's understanding of society is predicated on the assertion that human
beings are historical animals that create ontological forms.
History itself is the quintessence of this proposition. History is
a form of being; it animates a particular mode of existence, of
making a life. But it is also, at the same time, the domain within
which this creation of ontological form takes place. To be clear,
by "history" I am referring neither to some linear progressive notion of time defined by action nor to its reverse, the retrospective
assembly of inchoate events into a causal narrative—both being inventions of the imaginary of modernity. My sense of history would include any sort of "archaic" notions of temporal
circularity, simultaneity, or coincidence in the self-organization
of human time and space. No historical inquiry, in this respect, can be relieved of the burden of studying the capacity of
human beings to create and alter their world, for better or
worse. The human being is a historical animal because it creates its proper world in such a way that it can be accounted for
and organized into a corpus that can outlive its time frame of
living. The first order of such creation, thus fundamental and
outmaneuverable, is society itself, the edifice that signifies (which
is also to say, gives meaning to) the existence of the human
animal. But societies are not mere objects. Although they are
historical-ontological creations, they are simultaneously sources
of historical-ontological creation. Societies create their own
worlds in the course of time, in the full light (but not always
cognizance) of the fact that these worlds are always finite and
can be radically new, that is, radically other than those existing
worlds that make this othering possible. For Lefort, history is
discontinuity, and I will come back to this issue.

The political is one such historical-ontological element—a way that enables human beings to live, to organize and wage a life in the society that makes them be:

> The political is revealed, not in what we call political activity, but in the double movement whereby the mode of institution of society appears and is obscured, occulted. It appears in the sense that the process whereby society is ordered and unified across its divisions becomes visible. It is obscured in the sense that the space [*lieu*] of politics (the space in which parties compete and in which a general instantiation of power is formed and renewed) becomes defined as particular, while the principle which generates the overall configuration is concealed.[2]

The motif of visibility and invisibility is ubiquitous in Lefort's thought, an evident legacy of his mentor, Maurice Merleau-Ponty. We shall examine shortly in what sense this goes beyond mere phenomenological problems, but what is immediately striking here is that the political (*le politique*) is quintessentially implicated in this play of (in)visibility.[3] The political emerges out of the shadow play of the social. It is the backlight that animates the shadow theater, but also the canvas on which the

2. Claude Lefort, "The Question of Democracy," in *Democracy and Political Theory*, trans. David Macey (Minneapolis: University of Minnesota Press, 1988), 11. Translation modified.

3. Lefort follows the standard way in which contemporary French philosophy has distinguished the political (*le politique*) from politics (*la politique*). The latter is a sort of anthropological category for recognizing the existence of power in all human societies and the institutions that administer internal social conflict, while the former is the unique element that accounts for society's cognizant engagement with that condition. In other words, all societies bear a politics, but only some societies are political. Only Castoriadis, in his inimitable contrarian sensibility, uses the terms to refer to the same categorizations in reverse. For Castoriadis, *le politique* is the ubiquitous anthropological element, while *la politique* is the specific social-historical formation of a *poiëtic* praxis essential to a democratic society. See Castoriadis, "Democracy as Procedure and Democracy as Regime," in *Constellations* 4, no. 1 (1997): 1–18.

performance takes place. So the political comes to light when society comes together in spite of its unavoidable divisions, while it is occluded when society is reduced solely to its differential particularities at a specific point in the social space, thus concealing the generative principle that enables the configuration of social space to begin with. For Lefort, then, political thinking starts with the question "What is the nature of the difference between forms of society?" because, although the question of the political emerges along with the question of social formation (or the institution of society), the two questions can never be said to be identical. The political hinges on the handling of social differentiation. As a historical-ontological form, social formation (tribe, *polis*, empire, nation, communism, and so on) corresponds to a specific "anthropological" type, to a social imaginary, whose internal contestation and differentiation, however, become significant (which is also to say, signified) in the manifestation of the political.

But the political is not a mere vehicle of the expression of the social, nor can it be located in the contours of a specific social description, strictly speaking. Lefort explicitly deploys the political "to refer to the principles that generate society, or more accurately, different forms of society," and it is precisely "because the very notion of society already contains within it a reference to its political definition that it proves impossible to localize the political *in* society."[4] In other words, the political pertains to the generative principles of society as such: the forms created/configured to account for (but also, in that sense, to produce) the markers of social division and the inevitable internalization of those markers—inevitable because "*social division* can only be defined—unless of course we posit the absurd idea that it is a division between alien societies—insofar as it represents an internal division" (218). Internalization is

4. Claude Lefort, "The Permanence of the Theologico-Political?," in *Democracy and Political Theory*, 217. Translation modified where necessary. This work is hereafter cited in the text.

differentiation, to take it even further, in the sense that different forms register their difference when they accept it or embody it, when they make it internal to their existence. This is not to be understood as an organic, unmediated, or evolutionary process that aspires to some sort of consolidation. Social division registers itself in the process of an internally conducted configuration that (1) does not happen once and for all but is always open to reconfiguration and (2) happens always in specific historical conditions—conditions that shape it and yet are shaped by it.

Lefort famously argues that the terrain of both the historical-ontological genesis of societies and their political manifestation bears a specific geometry of three configurative modes: the conjuncture of what he calls *mise en forme* (forming/shaping—this is a *poiētic* notion); *mise en scène* (staging/realizing—this is a theatrical and perhaps practical notion in the sense that *praxis* is different from *poiēsis*); and *mise en sens* (creating/realizing meaning, which is both *poiētic* and practical). Of the three, the last is a neologism borrowed from the psychoanalytic theory of Piera Aulagnier, whose radical research in psychotic communication showed, unlike the claims of standard psychiatric assessments, that psychotics in fact do create language and do produce meaning, even if it is signifiable only in their own terms.[5]

Although this three-part modality pertains to the creation of all societal forms, it is particularly dramatic in the configuration of modernity. Lefort's thesis, roughly speaking, is that modernity comes as a new historical-ontological form, even if by mutation: an other social imaginary (this would be the poietic *mise en forme*), an other framework of social realization (this would be the theatrical/practical *mise en scène*), and an other way of creating meaning for itself (this would be the signifying

5. Piera Aulagnier, *The Violence of Interpretation: From Pictogram to Statement* (New York: Routledge, 2001).

mise en sens). The essential content of this proposition, for Lefort, is that modernity is the social-historical form that realizes
the political. Society no longer remains in a closed circuit where
the symbolic and the real coexist in a stable network of meaning, but enters a kind of existential rift: The symbolic and the
real are distended by a kind of primary void. In obvious historical terms, this void appears precisely because the double body
of the king is severed from its head—both the crown (symboli-
cally) and the actual head (altogether literally).[6]

There is much to say here about the figure of the body, but it
would lead us elsewhere. Certainly, for Lefort, the figure of the
popular body politic in modern democracy does not substitute
for the king's two bodies. Whatever the discussion about the
uncertainties of secularization, there is an arithmetic incom-
mensurability here: the multitude cannot be divided into two.
Moreover, the symbolic universe of democracy is constitutively
worldly, and this worldliness cannot be fissured. I am not
saying that the multitude evades metaphysics. Its metaphysics
becomes perceptible precisely insofar as it desires to become
one, but because this is constituted as self-denial of its social
differentiation—totalitarianism, for Lefort, is an outcome of
democracy's internal antagonism—the multitude's desired

6. Following Michelet, Lefort speaks of the fact that parading the captive
Louis XVI before the people makes visible the body of the king in such a way
that it entails a humanization that makes the transgression of regicide even
more traumatic (245–46). Philippe Roger, a renowned French historian of
this period, argues the contrary: Louis XVI loses access to his symbolic body
when he begins to adopt the language that challenges the ancien régime, even
before the storming of the Bastille. When the king addresses, in mere speech,
the issue of *les classes priviligiées*, he has automatically entered the domain of
the people, and when he is finally (re)named Citizen Capet, his execution is
a matter of course—the perils of citizenship. I am suggesting that we keep
these two interpretations in juxtaposition. See Philippe Roger, "Le débat de la
'langue révolutionnaire,'" in *La Carmagnole des Muses: L'Homme de lettres et
l'artiste dans la Révolution*, ed. Jean-Claude Bonnet (Paris: Armand Colin,
1988), 157–84.

monarchical symbol, unlike the desire of royalty, can never be divided into two bodies, worldly and otherworldly. The pillar slogan of modern democracy, "We, the People," retains this untenable grammar. The singular plural is an internally antagonistic figure, but it remains peculiarly indivisible in the very process of fostering and sustaining a demand for social differentiation. Although this contradiction is maddening from the perspective of enacting a radical democratic politics, nonetheless, we need to distinguish the metaphysics of oneness that this figure may provoke or bring about from the classic monotheistic metaphysics that precedes it in traditional monarchy.

The crux of Lefort's argument in "The Permanence of the Theologico-Political?" is really the attempt to theorize the terms and significance of this distinction. The question mark in the title should not be taken lightly. Grammatically, of course, it signifies the interrogation of permanence, but I would like to add that it also casts a shadow on the notorious hyphenated figure. What *is* the figure of the "theologico-political"? What sort of figure is it? Or, in other words, what is the domain of its performativity? Insofar as it is a figure, does its rhetorical constitution extend to social reality—that is, beyond mere rhetoric? I confess that I am uncertain whether it does. In any case, I would much rather see extensive inquiry into political theology as rhetoric than reiterations of the presumed authority of its reality. If nothing else, the advent of modernity demands that we interrogate the tacit harmony of the composite figure of "political theology" not only by imagining a politics that is no longer theological, but also by creating a framework of critique focused on the political history of theology. Imagining a nontheological politics goes hand in hand with deconstructing the political in theology.

Consider Lefort's question: "Can we say that religion has simply been erased from the face of politics (and remains only in the periphery of politics) without asking ourselves what its investment in the political order once meant?" (215). The insinuation is "Of course not," but to interrogate the erstwhile

investment of religion in the political order is itself the result
of conceiving the political beyond the theological. How is
this configured? The political is tantamount to the self-
representation of society in the symbolic sphere—a self-
symbolization, if we may say it that way—and not society's
representation via an externally constituted authority (the divine king), and therefore an externally constituted symbology.
On the other hand, Lefort also claims, "Every religion *states* in
its own way that human society can only open on to itself by
being held in an opening it did not create." He hastens to add
immediately, "Philosophy says the same thing, but religion said
it first, albeit in a language that philosophy cannot accept as its
own" (222). He says this in order to expose traditional philosophy's incapacity to accept the fact that on its own transcendental claims, it merely follows the transcendental claims of
religion, thus rendering philosophy's critique of religion ambivalent at best, if not disingenuous and self-serving (223). In
this sense, Lefort revokes philosophy's hold on determining the
political from the standpoint of categorical certainty, which
results in the bona fide occlusion of the political. In language
derived from Merleau-Ponty, Lefort argues over and over that
the political occurs when and where politics becomes visible.
In what has become a signature gesture, he recognizes and
situates this occurrence as the social-imaginary emergence of
modernity and the advent of democracy—the "democratic invention," as he calls it.[7]

Like modernity—or perhaps, more accurately, as modernity—
democracy entails a unique mode of societal *mise en forme*, and
Lefort makes it very clear that this formation has no models,
even if it may be said to have a heritage (225). Of course, he is
speaking of "modern democracy," and, at least in this context,
he shows little interest in making use of this heritage, which
we presume refers to the ancients and not to Machiavelli,

7. Claude Lefort, *L'Invention démocratique* (Paris: Fayard, 1981).

whom he studied exhaustively as a precursor. Before we criticize this privileged distinction of the modern, it is important to understand his configuration of it. The visibility of politics lies at the crux of the matter. All societies bear some sort of semantics of "self-externality" that enables them to have a quasi-representation of themselves, at the very least so as to safeguard the existential uniqueness of their institutions against the permanent threat posed by their enemies, the institutions of the other. How this self-externality is configured is built into society's institutions; it is an essential element of a specific mode of social organization. The overwhelming tendency of most societies in history—such that it constitutes a norm—is to conceal any traces of the instituting self so as to establish the certainty of externality, which thereby sustains itself with imperviously independent symbolic power. Often, one might say that this concealment of the self is achieved by an extraordinary sublimation. All nationalisms exemplify such a process, where the nation is the most coveted and existentially necessary sublimatory object for individuals who otherwise, without it, would be forlorn, with identities profoundly unstable and permanently threatened. Likewise, any notion of a "chosen people" (which at some level operates in all nationalisms)—manifest destiny, ancestral superiority, and so on—exemplifies such concealment of self via a sublimatory investment in some extrasocial outside, so that society's symbolic power is sealed in significations that remain untouched by the quotidian wear and tear of real history.

What is visible in such cases is the confirmation of the reality of heteronomy, which is, of course, as such, invisible to those who have authorized it. In heteronomy, society's foundational law (*nomos*) is not only real in its externality to the social; it is also real in its otherness. We can also say, at the same time, that it makes this otherness real in a tangible sense, in a sense that provides real comfort, streamlines troubled identities, and gives them real meaning. France is really a Republic; the American people really have an exceptional destiny; the

Greeks are really the ancestors of Western civilization; the Jews are really God's chosen people; and so on. For Lefort, modern democracy dismantles all that, first because, as he is often fond of saying, it "dissolves the ultimate markers of certainty," but also, more specifically, because it is "the only regime to have represented power in such a way as to show that power is an *empty place* [*lieu vide*] and to have thereby maintained a gap between the symbolic and the real" (225). This is not to say that in democracy power is nothing or is held by no one—although this is an issue I will return to at the end. It is to say that in democracy power belongs to no one, that nothing embodies it and no one can possess it, because in democracy power does not "refer to an *outside* that can be assigned to the gods, the City or the sacred ground [and] because it does not refer to an *inside* that can be assigned to the substance of the community" (226). The opposition of inside and outside here is not spatial, except in the most trivial sense. For even the inside is a bona fide outside, a self-configured externality from the most intimate internal elements—a self-configuration that, of course, conceals all aspects of the self, no matter how intimate or how internal they happen to be. That is, democracy puts an end to both "outside" and "inside" symbolic domains of power as domains of self-authorized (and simultaneously self-concealed) otherness. Therefore, in democracy "it is because there is no materialization of the *Other*—which would allow power to function as a mediator, however this is to be defined—that there is no materialization of the *One*—which would allow power to function as an incarnation" (226). The logical sequence of the sentence is important. While, say, in monotheistic thinking the privileged principle of the One is what animates the worship of an otherworldly Other (God is the One and Only Other), in democratic thinking, it is the incapacity even to materialize (not to mention worship) the Other that keeps it from slipping unto the reign of the One. Not only are these two imaginaries in opposition, but they are also characterized by a reverse causality.

There is yet another crucial consequence of this configuration, which for Lefort is one of the unprecedented aspects of the democratic imaginary. The dissolution of the ultimate markers of certainty and the visibility of power as an empty place repeal the instituted concealment of internal social division and differentiation by the guarantee of externalized power. Because democratic power can be given over wholly neither to the One nor to the Other, it becomes limited—or, more precisely, it reveals its limit—in the sense that it cannot exceed the field of contention from which it emerges and is authorized. Lefort is correct to say that democratic power "depends upon the institutionalization of conflict" (226), if we understand the notion of "institutionalization" not to signify some sort of freezing of movement in a symbolic edifice, juridical or governmental, but to retain the ever-renewable cauldron of contention that characterizes the polity. Even when various figures or symbols (e.g., the People, the Citizen, the Constitution) are invoked as agents of institutionalized universality, the field of contention (class struggle, sexual difference, ideological conflicts, inequities of all kinds) is never mastered, alleviated, or superseded. When attempts at mastery of social contention are being made, democracy is being defeated. The fact that, historically speaking, this happens practically as a norm may speak to the precariousness of democracy and perhaps to its ambivalent relation with violence, but it does not nullify its intrinsic politicization of contention. Democracy too is haunted by the incessant play of heteronomous desire, which sends it along paths of multiple paradoxes and unprecedented internal conflicts of its own.

Yet, drawing from the social-imaginary institution of modernity, democracy is the historical regime whose radical characteristic is to stage its internal conflicts openly for itself. On this stage, visibility and openness are paradoxically expressed in a *co-incident* veiling or concealing of their occurrence, a kind of openly conducted and self-instituted invisibility that Castoriadis (sharing his language with Lefort) has named "self-occultation." Before elaborating on this contradiction, it is useful to draw an elementary sketch of how Lefort sees this process taking place, unfolding the full triptych of *mise en forme–mise en scène–mise en sens*.

1. The social imaginary of modernity dismantles the closed symbolic circuit of premodern society by rendering visible the secrets of its performativity: the fact that the divine authority of the king is not divine at all but dependent on the consent of his subjects, who make this ruse visible the moment they re-voke their consent by realizing their ability to take off his head. Given the importance of embodiment of power in the ancien régime, this dismemberment of the Sovereign's body is more than just a symbolic act. What distinguishes the self-organization of society in modernity is the realization (in French, as a theatri-cal term, tantamount to *mise en scène*) of how real symbolic power actually is. This does not mean that the symbolic realm is abolished or rendered transparent. But it does mean that it loses its transcendental privilege to subsume the real. The con-sequence, in the other extreme, in what have been termed as so-cieties of postmodern capitalism, is that the ensuing incapacity to navigate the now-visible gap between the symbolic and the real facilitates the oblivious existence of depoliticized societies of consumerist addiction, but that is a whole other conversation.

2. The immediate consequence of this revolutionary *mise en scène* is the emergence of a new configuration of the space of power as a void in the symbolic constitution of authority be-cause, quite literally, there is no body in power.[8] Because, as I mentioned earlier, the People (as a revolutionary multitude) are too much of a differential and antagonistic plurality to simply move and be contained into the place of the One, the void be-comes a constitutive principle in turn, thereby producing an altogether radically other *mise en sens*—an entirely new

8. Bernard Flynn is correct to point out that the revolutionary moment in modernity is the disincarnation of power. See Bernard Flynn, *The Philosophy of Claude Lefort: Interpreting the Political* (Evanston, Ill.: Northwestern Uni-versity Press, 2005).

framework of meaning, which is furthermore marked by making visible a kind of primal meaninglessness of power. The meaninglessness of power is the shocking truth of revolution, so shocking that no revolution, historically speaking, has managed to avoid an almost instant repudiation of this truth by setting in motion its own machinery of filling the void with new transcendental meaning.

3. Although the creation of the political institutions we recognize as elemental to modern democracy surely derives from this new framework of meaning, the psychic sensors of society sustain society's recoiling in horror before this void, of whose visibility—one might even say, whose actuality—society recognizes itself to be the agent. So we have a self-recognition that paradoxically produces self-denial.[9] Admittedly, Lefort resists invoking a theory of the psyche in this configuration, so the terms "self-recognition" and "self-denial" should be read as formal structures. His explanation remains at the level of a certain generalized anthropology, perhaps considered still from a phenomenological standpoint: The void emerges from the noncoincidence of humanity with itself. This is a prepolitical substratum; the political emerges when this noncoincidence becomes visible and realizable in a specific imaginary (modernity) and a specific politics (democracy). Lefort's anthropological understanding of what may be seen as a prepolitical substratum— humanity's noncoincidence with itself—points to an intrinsic groundlessness or impossible foundation. It therefore resists any tendency toward transcendentalism. I can only concur

---

9. It occurs to me that the schema here parallels the figure of Kant recoiling before his discovery of the abyss of the imagination, which threatens the sovereignty of reason, as Heidegger famously pointed out in *Kant and the Problem of Metaphysics* (1929). But what tends to be forgotten in this story is Heidegger's recoil in turn as the problem of the abyssal imagination is overwritten by the ontology of *Dasein*. See Cornelius Castoriadis, "The Discovery of the Imagination," in *World in Fragments*, ed. David Ames Curtis (Stanford, Calif.: Stanford University Press, 1997), 213–45.

with Flynn's insightful observation that Lefort's anthropo-ontological standpoint is not driven by universalization but is akin to local knowledge.

4. As a result of this self-denial that seems to escort self-recognition, the void is thus concealed (again) by the very political institutions it fosters in the name of, for, and by the People: the Constitution, the Republic, the sphere of political parties, the realm of the law, and so on—that is, the entire framework of both canonical and agonistic constituencies that characterizes the new politics of democracy. I want to reiterate the significance of the French word *occultation*, common to both Lefort and Castoriadis, for the designation of this concealing as not just occluding but occulting oneself—that is, producing a new form of transcendental secrecy that veils the void. It would be absolutely misguided to consider this a matter of failed secularization, thinking à la Schmitt that the religious imaginary persists in secularized guise. Instead, we should emphasize that a new mode of heteronomy is fostered by the very recoiling before the abyss thus produced (or rather, unconcealed) by the Revolution, which can never be reduced to the heteronomy that preceded it.

5. To complete this crude sketch: The empty place of power, Lefort says, cannot be represented or even apprehended. Strictly speaking, it cannot be occupied, in the sense of being politically possessed. In the best of liberalism, it can be, as it were, rented out in turn: By consensus, elected political constituencies can move in and out of the place of power. When liberalism fails, a kind of impostor occupier emerges, the totalitarian personality. He is an impostor because, no matter what may be the elaborate rituals of totalitarianism's personality cult, the dictator never becomes divine.

In historical terms, we see in totalitarianism the extraordinary convergence of two things: society's recoiling in horror before its own responsibility to rule itself and, as a result, society's total consent to be ruled by the One, but as one of their own.[10] This difference between premodern monarchy and modern totalitarianism is crucial. It is a difference between contrary fictionalizations. Louis XIV was indeed One because he was one of a kind, an almost alien otherworldly figure in the way that Franz Kafka has sketched out the distant myth of the Chinese Emperor. The power of the *Führer*, on the other hand, was drawn from his embodiment of the German *Volk*; he acceded to the position of the One precisely because he was not one of a kind but "one of us," the essence of "us." Both involve elaborate mythistorical structures of support by the population that produce a self-abrogating mentality of obedience, even devotion, but the medieval imaginary that is still in effect in the era of Roi Soleil can be invoked only as a grotesque parody in the era of the Third Reich. One, of course, can object that the utterance "L'État, c'est Moi" already acknowledges the split of oneness signaled in the tautological proposition, as well as the worldliness of the self who speaks the name of the State (not dissimilar to Louis XVI's speaking the name of the privileged classes less than a century later). However, it is precisely the point that such reading of the utterance, such visibility of the reality of power, is foreclosed in a monarchical universe of meaning. (I am using the term "monarchy" literally: *Archē* is monological and as singular principle—of rule but also origin of rule—enshrouds society's differential field of vision.) In the modern totalitarian situation—but as a result of a different psychosocial process, as I mentioned—the monarchical universe of

10. There is an affinity of my claim here with Bernard Flynn's distinction that, although both are autocratic political authorizations, premodern monarchy is based on transcendental authority, while modern totalitarianism is based on immanent authority. I would add only that, like the outside/inside argument before, in heteronomy of any kind the immanent other is transcendentalized. As Lefort himself concludes, "In the theologico-political labyrinth . . . any move towards immanence is also a move toward transcendence" (254).

meaning returns to reign again, even if in grotesque simulation. The modern situation is, of course, more insidious, if one can possibly stage such comparisons, because it emerges out of democracy's self-concealed unraveling while retaining its populist undercurrent: To say that our Leader is one of us and therefore can command us absolutely is perhaps the most hideous, stupefying (and undoubtedly stupid) instance of what La Boétie named "voluntary servitude" in relation to monarchy. In modern terms, it is also the most dramatic indication of society's terror before the reality of the empty space of power.

Let me elaborate on the concrete implications of this reality by looking closely at Lefort's language. When a void in the place of power emerges, power is not voided. On the contrary, power may be said to emerge unadulterated, that is, groundless and unqualified, unfounded and uncertain. In the face of the empty place of power, society no longer sees itself unified in its affirmation. Rather, society "presents itself in the shape of an endless series of questions (witness the incessant, shifting debates between ideologies)" (228). This leads Lefort to elaborate that "modern democracy breaks down old certainties by inaugurating an experience where society resides in the quest for its own foundations" (229). My tendency immediately would be to add that this quest for self-foundation is futile—infinitely futile—because no foundation exists before or beneath this self in order to be discovered. A democratic imaginary makes society confront the fact of this futility of discovery, which as a result enables this 'self'—the self-determining and self-governing society that acts on its desire for autonomy—to create indeed a foundation: a Revolution, a Constitution, or what have you. If it does not recoil in self-denial, a self-determining and self-governing society cannot lose sight of the terrifying fact that the ground of its foundations is abyssal, that there is no ground, and that therefore this Revolution and this Constitution are themselves nothing but manifestations of society itself having become "an endless series of questions." Then this groundless self-foundation, as precarious as it is by necessity, may be said to provide, in provisionally affirmative terms, "something to be gained by calling the law into question, [the fact] that freedom is a conquest" (229).

Because Lefort's attention remains on the persistence of the theological element in politics, even if not at all in the manner of Schmitt and his contemporary followers in political theology, he does not extract from this stipulation its due. To say that freedom is a matter of conquest means automatically to efface any suggestion that freedom exists in nature or as foundation. There is, in other words, no freedom to be found, and surely no freedom to be founded by right. Freedom is the wager in the contentious field of interrogating the law. Its achievement is resolutely agonistic and cannot be granted the alibi of formal justification. There are no existential parameters that precede the social organization of humanity (Rousseau) or inalienable natural rights (Jefferson) that could, therefore, be called on to justify a revolutionary foundation in an emancipatory project or necessitate an institution of sovereignty (Hobbes) as protection against natural annihilating violence. To take seriously Lefort's consistent assertion of humanity's irreparable noncoincidence with itself means to revoke all possibility that the equation between law and freedom can be solved philosophically, outside the terrain of political contention. Onto this terrain, no one—no "self"—comes intact. The field of vision now marked by the void means that even the beholder becomes a site of interminable interrogation; the noncoincidence is now visible, indeed sentient, on the very ground of one's identity, which itself becomes "an endless series of questions."

But Lefort's analysis proceeds as if this condition of radical uncertainty is impossible or unfeasible. I would agree, of course, that it is intolerable, and the history of both individuals and societies—in democracy above all—suggests that it is unsustainable for long, that it recedes and cancels itself by the most elaborate constructions of new certainties—that it "surrenders to the attractions of regained certainty," Lefort says explicitly (234). This does not mean, however, that we give up the challenge to think and act out of uncertainty in real, concrete, political ways. And it certainly does not mean that because human beings relish their indulgence in inventing and constructing new certainties, we return inevitably to the interpretive framework established by what motivated "old certainties": religious desire. This is precisely the uninterrogated position of postsecularism: a self-righteous defense of religious desire as an allegedly nonideological and realist view of today's world, which in reality is actually an unimaginative, politically safe, and perfectly ideological position.

Certainly, I am not suggesting that Lefort is a post-secularist or that he can even be interpellated as one with any kind of scholarly credibility. Neither is he, of course, a Schmittian, as I have already said several times, not only because he thinks in terms of democracy but also because, on this specific point, he does not at all share Schmitt's genuine theological desire. Moreover, no Schmittian and no post-secularist would tolerate such profound investment in the privileged historical rupture signaled by modernity. And it is modernity that is made to bear the most conceptual weight in this argument, more than democracy, politics, or religion. Lefort presents a complex and, I think, problematic argument on this point, which is, nonetheless, unique and not paid deserved attention by either the enemies or the advocates of modernity. Insofar as the modern revolutionary upheaval characterizes society's recognition and confrontation of a visible emptiness at the core of power, Lefort seems to opt for a theory of historical discontinuity, not unlike many of the radical French thinkers of his generation. But in seeking to account for the "postrevolutionary" tendency in modernity to recapture the magnetism of symbolic discourses of the One (by universalizing the politics of social difference), Lefort seems to entertain the idea of a sort of recurrent desecularization, a sort of a reincarnation of the religious in the midst of the void. In this respect, his argument for modernity's historical discontinuity reveals a curious ambivalence.

In much of my writing against post-secularist positions and their dispute of the secularization thesis, I have underlined, time and again, that secularization is not just unfinished but unfinishable by definition, and that just because residual religious elements abound in secular societies, it does not mean that the secular has not in fact set in motion an element of social-historical transformation, perhaps even radical transformation. This is why to equate the metaphysics of secularism with the metaphysics of religion is naïve and inaccurate, to say to the least. Lefort's analysis of Michelet's take on the French Revolution, impeccable though his scholarship is, nonetheless edges into this problematic territory. Unlike the standard post-secularist manipulation that sees religion everywhere and in everything secular, Lefort sees the epistemology of religious thinking lurking in the politico-philosophical epistemology that denies it. But even if we accept that this is the case—there is certainly a great deal of Christian pietism in Kantian transcendentalism, for example—can we simply restrict our account of whatever transcendental (or at the extreme limit, totalitarian) tendencies develop out of the void of modernity to some sort of reactivation of the religious in whatever disguise? Is this not, in the end, Carl Schmitt's thesis, even if it is arrived at in reverse? Is it satisfactory enough, as a theoretical argument, to say that Christianity may not be residual in secularized modernity but is nonetheless the pattern by which this modernity creates its own metaphysics—in the same way in which Michelet, for example, judges "the mystical conception of the Revolution" to be "modeled on Christ's appearance on earth" (240)? Does it really matter whether Christianity is a residual imaginary or a model imaginary? Is there really a difference?

Past his digression on Michelet, as he calls it, Lefort moves into a conclusion that compromises the essay's initial elaborations on what enables the visibility of the empty space of power. He raises a dilemma "whether democracy is the theater of a new mode of transference or whether the only thing that remains in it is the phantom of the theologico-political" (249). He then proceeds to argue, without question, that "the ideas of reason, justice, and right, which inspire both a return to the principles of classical thought and a movement toward a secularized ethic, are themselves caught in a theologico-political elaboration" in order to conclude with a series of similes between the secular-modern and the Christian-medieval political modes and institutions, whose crowning phrase is "Justice, like Christ, becomes an object of worship [*culte*]" (251). There is a surprising lack of interrogation at this stage of the essay. No doubt, like any other social imaginary in history, secular modernity is not immune to modalities, practices, and symbols of worship. No doubt, given the history of European and European-derived societies, the signs of worship most often bear direct Christian references, which are assumed tacitly and reproduced unquestionably by the population. As a result, no one would seriously claim, for example, that the stamp "In God We Trust" on the U.S. dollar is referring to the God of Money. Yet, to be accurate, this is the only god that can be said to exist in a world where the dollar itself is the supreme object of worship, and in whose name, value, and pursuit whole societies may be destroyed many times over. The assumed and unquestioned Christian reference is actually nothing but concealment (occultation) of this fact. Indeed, it is a concealment of something even more profound, perhaps intolerable: the fact that in secular modernity, symbols of worship, regardless of the names, are made visible as the idolatrous acts they always are—they always have been. Why should a philosopher say so easily that "Justice, like Christ, becomes an object of worship" and genuinely believe that "Christ" is the requisite reference when "Christ"—and any other such name, even what is often barred from being named—is nothing but an idol. Imagine how different would be the meaning of this alleged "theologico-political elaboration" of secular modernity if the phrase read "Justice, like an idol, becomes an object of worship."

Not fully addressing the aporias of "this brief excursion into the theologico-political labyrinth," as he calls it (254), Lefort closes the essay by returning to his radical assertions about the democratic invention in modernity. A succinct description of the condition that, in his words, "breaks down the mechanisms of incarnation" ensues: "The disincorporation of power is accompanied by the disincorporation of thought and by the disincorporation of the social" (255). We have returned to the initial image of rupture that makes the king's two bodies vanish and replaces them with no body at all. The question of how democracy can emerge from the corporatist model of monarchical society is not answered in terms of any sort of framework of determination. The void in power is both event and evidence of discontinuity. Lefort here reiterates that if we keep the tension between the religious and the political in play at all, it would mean that literally a transformation has taken place that has exploded them from within in the sense that

> [a] transfer from one register to the other [was] intended to ensure the preservation of a *form* which has since been abolished, that the theological and the political became divorced [*dénoués*], that a new experience of the institution of the social is configured [*dessinée*], that the religious is reactivated in the weak and failing points [*points de défaillance*] of the social, that its efficacy is no longer symbolic but imaginary and that, ultimately, it is an expression of the unavoidable—and no doubt ontological—difficulty democracy has in reading its own story [*à se rendre lisible pour elle-même*]. (255)

I admit that I don't know whether the reactivation of religion in the modern democratic imaginary (even if it is correctly said to be "in the weak and failing points of the social") is the expression of democracy's difficulty in reading its own story, of making itself readable to itself, but I am certain of the reality of this difficulty, although I hasten to add that paradoxically it exists in a political formation that is more keen on (perhaps even obsessed with) reading—and writing—itself, its own story, than any other in the history of human societies. Lefort's own story about the advent of democracy in modernity may itself be an expression of difficulty in reading oneself. According to his account, it is modernity that enables the emergence of democracy, not the other way around. This radical historicity of the modern begs the question of Athenian democracy as a form. I surely don't mean to suggest that Athenian democracy is some sort of primary form or some sort of model. But its actual historical existence, even in the context of archaic societies, cannot be disregarded as a formative force. Although democracy in Athens dies—all social and historical forms are finite—the social imaginary of the democratic *polis* retains its force as a kind of wandering phantasm. We have seen its occasional (and always ephemeral and partial) reemergence in various historical instances, from the Italian Renaissance cities to American town councils, from the Paris Commune to workers' councils, anarchist governance, and so on—whenever we see the emergence of self-institution and self-government. The question to ask is this: How do we account for the work of this phantasm in the revolutionary situation that Lefort describes? Given that the phantasm wanders still, we certainly cannot discount its presence in that story.

If democracy is thus not merely the child of modernity, but a phantasm that leans on the social-imaginary process by which modernity is actualized, we might want to question whether the void of modernity may not indeed be a new historical formation. Here we would want to return to the psycho-ontological substratum that underlies the political manifestation of society, which enacts—but does not at all determine in some causal sense—humanity's entrance into history. From this standpoint, the void of political power is always there. It signifies the very being of society's institution. The figure of the king's two bodies is but a particular form of concealment of the void, which presents a full incarnation of power. Although this symbolic order proved relatively stable in medieval Europe, we have a great deal of pre-Enlightenment material from Machiavelli to Montaigne, La Boétie, and Spinoza that testifies, in various terms, to the recognition that this incarnation was an illusion and that its concealed worldliness was its primary constitutive horizon. Whether and how the wandering phantasm of ancient democracy played a role in these realizations is worth discussing.

Whatever would be the conclusion of such a discussion, the inquiry would show that the lesson conducted by the Athenians was that the empty space of power can indeed be occupied—which is not to say filled, possessed, or abolished as a void—by the *polis* in its entirety, in its differential multiplicity, which does not have to be unified into one. This is why the only possible condition for keeping the void unconcealed is to sustain a form of radical democracy in which representation (both symbolic and institutional, as in representative democracy) is continuously undermined by the internally antagonistic presence of the *dēmos*. Crudely speaking, democracy cannot take place in secret; it requires the uninterruptible visibility of the *dēmos*, and this cannot be sustained if the *dēmos* is concealed in its own representation. A visible *dēmos* that remains readable to itself would mean that the empty or abyssal space of democracy itself remains uninterruptibly visible. But it also means that in the purest light of the void, the unconcealed space of power is nonetheless visibly occupied by the *dēmos* in full cognizance of the (prepolitical) groundlessness that underlies it. Democracy, in its radical sense, is the only regime where the void is occupied unconcealed.

This may be said to have been present in effect in the symbolic language of the Occupy movement, which emerged, after all, from the actual occupation of public spaces rendered void to a public that has lost its capacity to read itself as a public. At its best, the assembly movement that found itself in the streets, squares, parks, and other public spaces in various cities of the world since 2010 operated in full light of the empty space of power. Even if there was tangible recognition and precise naming of the savage oligarchy that claims the space of power as its own, the public's withdrawal of consent could be predicated only on the recognition that the self-proclaimed entitlement of oligarchy is groundless, that it rests on a void. However, as the subsequent setback in most ranks of these movements showed, the problem of terror upon the realization of this recognition remains unsolved.[11] No radical democratic movement can aspire to political success unless it can imagine itself in government in full cognizance of the underlying void at the core of power that can never be repealed. In order to be actualized, such imagining of oneself in government would have to remain unencumbered by the revolutionary phantasms of the past, which exist in order to fill the void, and without the least bit of guilt for having to sustain the liberty of democracy by assuming the full administration of the law in the name of self-government— autonomy and isonomy—beyond the established limits of (neo) liberal juridical and governmental practice. Radical democracy cannot exist without creating a new governmentality. This is the crucial task at hand.

11. This is the case even when it is revealed by mistake, as in the instance of Clint Eastwood's notorious performance at the 2012 Republican National Convention, where he addressed the president of the United States as an empty chair. Even Eastwood's own constituency found the image abhorrent, and certainly not because Republicans have been known lately for their respect toward the office of the president. A satisfactory attack on Obama by his enemies could never take place against his conjured absence; it requires the full visibility of his body, all the more since, in this case, the attack is animated by inveterate racism. The unabashed rendering of the Invisible Man on stage was, in this latter sense, mind-boggling—all at once, as brutal irony, shameless self-disclosure, and political incapacity.

SIX

Responding to the Deregulation of the Political

I remember the devastating irony of a *New York Times* front-page photograph on Thanksgiving Day 2011 depicting a row of people who had pitched tents outside a Best Buy department store in Mesquite, Texas. Alas, the campers were not staging an Occupy Best Buy but positioning themselves at the head of the Black Friday mad rush. At any other time, the photograph would have been unremarkable, perhaps not even newsworthy. This itself shows how extensively consumerist desire is internalized in the American psyche, and how ingrained Black Friday (what an utterly cynical name!) has become in American life that it now occupies a slot in society's calendar. In fact, this year (2012) Black Friday was pushed back into Thanksgiving Thursday evening, at the limit of people's all too likely indigestion, because no calendar of feasts can withstand the panic for commodities. Selling Christmas trees on Labor Day is hardly unimaginable. Some years ago, a person died on Black Friday, trampled in the mad storming of a Walmart palace in New Jersey. I remember at the time arguing that charges should be brought against President George W. Bush for instigating homicide because on the day after 9/11 he had commanded the American people to respond to the catastrophe by going shopping.

This nexus of images and references encapsulates today's social predicament. A population addicted to the ephemeral pleasures of commodity consumption has become a toy in the hands of ruthless profiteers who are driving it recklessly to irreversible impoverishment, while politicians and demagogues of all kinds triumphantly proclaim their commitment to defend this "American way of life" at all costs from virtual enemies, internal and external. Although some discussion about "cost" has been seeping upward into the country's consciousness, the pattern remains difficult to break, not only because of what is evidently a social addiction to commodification but also because people have been all the more conditioned to respond to fear and catastrophe (even imminent bankruptcy or total impoverishment) by going shopping.

Most of the 99 percent in the United States are still more ready to go shopping than to go protesting—this we must acknowledge in order to move ahead to any substantial political assessment. Whatever effect the Occupy movement may have had so far can be assessed only in light of this realization. Various radically altering experiences have emerged from participating in Occupy actions throughout the country, but if any one of them would matter above all others, it would have to be the collective reversal of consumerist training and the reorientation of social desire to alternative kinds of actions that denigrate the entire paradigm of commodified life, the imperative to atomized values of private exclusionary enjoyment. I know that this is not the language most used in this discussion, but people's actions in the Occupy movement—from the emphasis on collective (re)education in radical democratic values to such direct action as transferring their money out of major investment banks into credit unions—speak to this effect: Real democratic politics can be conducted only against capitalist values.

I am now convinced that of the many dimensions permeating assembly movements worldwide—not just Occupy Wall Street (OWS) but also the movements in the Arab world, Spain, Greece, and elsewhere—the central dimension is the opposition between democracy and capitalism. Nothing else is of consequence. There are many particulars that merit specific examination, reflection, and assessment, but they are all particulars (regardless of cultural or social-historical differences) of one substantial generality: Whatever happens in today's world, which may decide irreversibly the future of the planet, is the consequence of an overt struggle between democracy and capitalism. For this reason, liberalism is no longer useful as a domain of significations pertinent to present social-historical reality. At best, historically speaking, liberalism sought to overcome the contradiction between democracy and capitalism by forging an ideological adhesion between them under the rubric exemplified by Benjamin Constant's more precise rendering of the American imperative to "the pursuit of happiness": Liberty consists in the institutional guarantee of our private pleasures.[1] This became the dominant mind-set for both "modernized" societies and those allegedly seeking "modernization." From this standpoint, neoliberalism is neither a new formation nor an aberrant branch of liberalism that can be corrected so as to return to the road of political and economic self-regulation.

If we take neoliberalism seriously not simply as economics but as world theory, then no doubt Jean-François Lyotard's assertion that the epoch of grand or master narratives has passed is wrong. In the very narrow sense that Lyotard's assertion was made in the midst of neoliberalism's ascendancy to triumph and hegemony, the fact that he did not perceive it as a master narrative of his own time—the master narrative that his theory against master narratives was unable to defy—raises all kinds

---

1. This is the essence of Constant's liberalism as argued in his famous pamphlet "The Liberty of the Ancients Compared to That of the Moderns" (1816).

of questions. These questions cannot be specifically addressed here, but we are pressed to wonder in what sense neoliberalism is indeed a formation that may be said to perpetuate or to restage—and the question of difference, alteration, or newness would be critical here—master narratives. With regard to economic practice, neoliberalism surely has a long and composite history that includes the "embedded liberalism" it allegedly overcame (both Keynesianism and the neoclassical liberalism of the Chicago school that opposed it), as well as the most obvious economics landmarks since the 1970s: Reaganomics, Thatcherism, Milton Friedman's apotheosis of Hong Kong economics, Japanese privatization, the incredibly named "Pinochet miracle," the cornucopia of World Bank and International Monetary Fund shenanigans (first in the underdeveloped world and former Soviet societies, then in Asia and South America, and now in southern Europe), all the way, of course, to the salient disaster of what we have come to call by different names: financial capitalism, economic deregulation, or globalization.

This is the trajectory of "the Global Minotaur," as the economist Yanis Varoufakis has aptly named it.[2] In a groundbreaking analysis that serves as a beacon in navigating today's political-economic mire, Varoufakis traces the trajectory of the current financial crisis from the decision by the United States in 1971 to effectively dismantle the Bretton Woods agreement (1944) that until then had governed an international recirculation of surplus wealth, thereby keeping in check capitalism's endemic tendency to unbounded expansion at all costs. Richard Nixon's decision to disengage the U.S. economy from the gold standard unleashed the subsequent determination of all currency by fiat, thus enabling unprecedented and reckless manipulation by all the national players in the international

2. Yanis Varoufakis, *The Global Minotaur: America, the True Origins of the Financial Crisis and the Future of the World Economy* (New York: Zed Books, 2011).

currency market. Emerging as the world's dominant economy after World War II, the U.S. economy established a new modus operandi of deficit wealth, that is, a national economy model no longer based on producing and circulating one's own surplus wealth but, as Varoufakis argues, circulating the surplus wealth of others. In this sense, the U.S. economy became a double beneficiary: It configured itself as an unprecedented consumer's market that absorbed the world's manufacturing at extraordinary scale and speed and, at the same time, as an all-around investment bank space that multiplied the profit capital of the world's producers with significant profit margins for itself. Hence the creation of a double society of equally insatiable mass consumers and elite financiers, whose complicity gave new meaning to "the pursuit of happiness" while bolstering the politics of liberal oligarchy that came to be known as neoliberalism.

But whatever may be the bona fide changes in economic practices in capitalism's past fifty years, the overarching social imaginary is still very much at work. Hence the scandalous silence about the negligent disregard of neoliberalism's immanent affinities with the classical origins of liberalism exemplified in the writings of Adam Smith, who, let us not forget, put forth not a theory of economics but a moral philosophy, that is, a world theory. After all, neoliberalism still feeds on the classic liberal notion of self-regulation—always an outrageous misnomer—under the name "deregulation," which is conducted on the basis of producing, that is, *forcibly extracting from the market*, greater self-regulation—language here plunging head-on into nonsense. Self-regulation is conventionally signified by Smith's classic metaphor "the invisible hand of the market"— which is perhaps invisible but is nonetheless a hand. The "free" market depends on its regulation so the norm of its "freedom" can be guaranteed. Deregulation was invented in the name and service of self-regulation, and deficit wealth was its deliberate outcome. Alan Greenspan, its celebrated maestro, justified this explicitly, even when, in utter cynicism, he accepted it as an ideological flaw in the aftermath of the banking collapse in 2008.[3]

"Deregulation" is an outrageously deceptive name. It defines a decision made and backed by political institutions, a brutal market intervention. Even in strict economic terms, deregulation concerns specific (partial and stealth) regulation—that is, invisible rules (in the name of no rules) whose purpose is not only to maximize control of the game by those who gain from it but also to exterminate those who oppose them. In other words, it is elementary monopoly capitalism, but at an unprecedented magnitude and scale—*naked capitalism*, as the name of a popular blog has it. There is similar newspeak concerning another pillar of neoliberalism: privatization. What is privatization but the production of new sorts of publics in the name of allegedly enhancing private/individualist opportunity? "Publics" is an inadequate word because of the outrageous scale of population numbers. We are talking about mass enclaves produced by consumer compulsion or mass migration—publics of an altogether other order than the power of constituencies in classic eighteenth-century liberal politics, but nonetheless publics in the name of the same social imaginary of geographic expansion, social mobility, and technical mastery.

So, whatever the economics of so-called neoliberalism, its politics matters most. And this politics exemplifies the endemic incompatibility between democracy and capitalism. What characterizes the current situation is what can be named, in full cognizance of the deceptive naming, "the deregulation of the political." Strictly speaking, deregulation of the political favors those who claim to be beyond the political and, to their benefit, apply extraordinary political control otherwise invisible to the overt political process. This beyond is occupied by what is

---

3. See Edmund L. Andrews, "Greenspan Concedes Error in Regulation," *New York Times*, October 23, 2008, http://www.nytimes.com/2008/10/24/business/economy/24panel.html.

an equally occult term: "market forces." In saying this, I obviously do not wish to revert to some sort of economic determinism. On the contrary, I think that against the inordinate punditry of experts about the market's difficulties in a debt-driven economy, it is the palpable power of market forces that we are dealing with, a power that is, by definition (as power), political. Perhaps one of the essential slogans by which this power expressed itself in overt political fashion was the famous beacon of the second Bill Clinton presidential campaign: "It's the economy, stupid!"—a slogan that literally reconfigures the "stupid" political subject as an object of an economic command.[4] Moreover, as the drive to disassemble the social democratic state in Europe and the United States seems paramount, and thereby the very capacity of society to respond to this power is under question, we can speak, not inaccurately, of a prolonged deregulation of the political, whose tangible outcome is that the electorate now figures as an inchoate body of renegade and uncontrolled self-interest. There are different dimensions of this phenomenon, depending on the sociocultural and historical occasion, from identity politics to ideological clientelism, which I will not discuss here, except to say that they are actually symptoms of this deregulation. Alas, these symptoms of disparate microinterest that splinters the social body are often taken as safeguards of the political.

The presumption that the inextricable nexus of the economic with the political is disengageable and that the two ought to remain independent of each other has long served the employment of experts and media town criers worldwide. Yet no matter how this situation may be expertly spun, not since the Weimar period (speaking in a European time frame) have we seen such a crisis of the political—a crisis of the overt signification of the

4. This is expertly argued by Athena Athanasiou in her extensive essay on the biopolitical dimensions of the current situation both globally and specifically in Greece. See *The Crisis as "State of Exception"* (Athens: Savvalas, 2012), 17–19.

political, which in democratic societies minimally consists of
the active engagement of the public with the law for the purposes of law's (re)examination and alteration if needed. I emphasize "overt" because otherwise, as a result of the "deregulation"
I mentioned, the sphere of the political has never been more
cryptically permeated and actualized by other domains—chiefly
the economic, but also multiple domains of mass-media technologies. So as not to be misunderstood, in speaking of a crisis,
I do not mean retreat of the political or inhabiting the 'post-
political' or any other such nonsense. What I mean concretely
is this: No banker, no finance minister, no international CEO,
no speculator, no hedge-fund manager, no public relations firm,
no mass-media director, no market pundit, no major economist in the university or the public sphere, in thinking, writing, or deciding about the debt crisis today, is engaged in
anything but wielding political power.

Although, since Marx, we have definitively known that economic interests ultimately determine the political trajectory of
societies, we now see economic agents explicitly exercising governmental power. Never mind the well-documented control of
U.S. government officials by Wall Street lobbyists; witness the
unelected prime ministers of Greece and Italy in 2011–12 earn-
ing their high-ranking qualifications at the European Central
Bank. In the United States, this condition is bolstered by the
very arm of the law. Note the three outrageous names of the
new American legality: *Citizens United, Right to Work, Stand
Your Ground.* These names are relentlessly cruel; they mock the
very polity they depoliticize by law with utter cynicism. The
U.S. Supreme Court has legalized the annihilation of citizenship by legislating in favor of the citizen's economic, not political, determination. And laws in various states have annihilated
the rights of working citizens by legalizing their *Right to Work
for Nothing* or have subjugated human life to the sovereignty of
a gun in the name of private property and at the behest of the
weapons industry. That this is currently the dominant mode
of *political* power and yet remains unperceived, ignored, or

disavowed as such is overtly indicative of the deregulation of the political.

The economic reconfiguration of the political resides at the core of globalization. We see a broad phenomenon of elected governments either unable to combat market invasions (being often at the mercy of credit-rating agencies, as if nations are corporations) or bought straight out by powerful financial conglomerates. No doubt, the capitulation of such governments has been enabled by the tacit consent of the majority of the population, which was sold (in more ways than one) to the pipe dream of economic prosperity and consumerist comfort. But as international bankers and financiers margin themselves out in a relentless race of greed for capital accumulation, real wealth is summarily removed from households across the board, homes are lost, savings and retirement accounts are pillaged, and insurmountable debt becomes the new national economy. All the while, global conglomerates continue to rake in record profits, and leading executives of banks and corporations continue to reward themselves with ever-higher bonuses as master traders of debt. It is in this sense that investment banking becomes highway robbery, and it is regrettable that one cannot but relish the brilliant verse that Bertolt Brecht gives to Mack the Knife in *The Threepenny Opera* (1928): "What's robbing a bank compared to founding a bank!" Mackie's sardonic declaration from the heart of Weimar reality exemplifies the quintessential principle of financial capitalism in the twenty-first century: kleptocracy. Banks have free reign to gamble with people's deposited savings or mortgaged properties, but while they keep billions of profits for themselves, they saddle people with billions of losses from their reckless bets. States then implement austerity programs, which are essentially no more than ways of cashing in on such losses as whole countries become enslaved to debt relations at loan-shark rates. At the closing of 2012, the finance and investment journal *Barron's* ran a full front page photograph of a mass demonstration of unemployed people in Spain with the unabashedly cynical headline: "Europe—Time to Buy." Kleptocracy is the language of the crisis, and the crisis is not economic but political.[5]

Bankers and financiers worldwide, with the support of servile media, have established the language of numbers as the only language of truth, while at the same time their irresponsible manipulation of numbers have sent entire populations, real men, women, and children, to ruin. But a battle against society's incapacitation cannot be calculated and conducted in the language of numbers, at least not in numbers that accumulate in the data banks of computers. It takes place in the sphere of social struggle and the political capacity of a people who come together in the actual numbers of bodies to determine (and alter) their own ways.

Any contemporary discussion of radical politics in the present juncture of this deregulation of the political must be conducted in light of recent international events that may be said to have begun with what has been dubbed "the Arab Spring" and were followed by what was called the "assembly movement" primarily seen in the public squares of Spain and Greece in the summer of 2011, and in turn by what was named the "Occupy movement" in the United States, starting with action in New York against the politics of Wall Street. All these namings are rather cavalier, but the magnitude of the events is indisputable, even as their manifestations are currently dissipating or shifting into more typified political relations of power, either of apathy or of violence. In essence, the overt political demand has been the same, despite differences in social-historical givens or geocultural specifics: The people as a whole must take over the political means and must do so outside established

---

5. See Raimundo Viejo, "Kleptocracy: Debt as a Method of Legalized Robbery," trans. Richard McAleavey, http://roarmag.org/2012/07/raimundo -viejo-kleptocracy-debt-crisis/ [originally published in *Diagonal* 179 (2012): 33]. For a concrete case in detail, see Matt Taibbi, "The Scam Wall Street Learned from the Mafia," *Rolling Stone* 1160/1161 (July 5–19, 2012): 80–88.

political institutions, which have effectively betrayed their avowed responsibility to represent and enact the people's will by serving explicitly the financial interests of economic elites. Against the bankruptcy of parliamentary institutions, the voiced demand has been for "direct democracy"—in Greek particularly relevant as "unmediated" (*amesē*) democracy, which also invokes simultaneously the sense of urgency: "immediate." This demand is actually the demand for democracy as such, for democracy is either direct democracy or is nothing—other than some form of oligarchy, narrow or broad, totalitarian or liberal.

The assembly movement, as a specific mode of political agonistics of indignation—following the call of *Indignez Vous!* (2010), the best-selling pamphlet by French Resistance elder Stéphane Hessel—is a direct response to this situation. It epitomizes what will become the major battlefield of future decades, democracy against capitalism, all the more because it aims at a politics that starts outside established political institutions that falsify democracy in the service of capitalism. This battlefield is not a matter of contingency, which would determine a position according to some sort of strategic preference. Deciding on democracy versus capitalism is not a matter of choice. It is a structural antagonism that cannot be structurally resolved or overcome from within the structure as it currently stands. Moreover, no subject position is ever possible outside this antagonism—except to the degree that we conceptualize it and articulate it in language. Therefore, we face the paradoxical situation of being pressed to form dissenting modalities that challenge the sovereignty of existing political avenues, to the degree that this sovereignty bolsters the sovereignty of capitalism. As the actual space of political institutions becomes ever more violated, degraded, and indeed occupied by the power of financiers, while the electoral process, not to mention the legal process, is increasingly manifested as a mechanism of disenfranchisement and subjugation, the only viable option for a real democratic political space becomes the street. Surely, this specific gesture is nothing new. It has been historically the last option when the subjugation of peoples reaches a certain threshold of accommodation. This threshold is quite elastic, which is why it rarely snaps, but when it does, it mobilizes a breakout of rage.

It's difficult to pinpoint the difference between indignation and rage; surely, the name *los indignados* echoes the legacy of *les enragés*. Indignation is proper to the present situation, considering also that the demand for dignity (*karama*) was the collective cry in the Arab Spring. However, the politics of assembly movements cannot be altogether disengaged from other spontaneous actions of enraged civil unrest, such as the banlieues riots in Paris (2005), the December uprising in Athens and other Greek cities (2008), or the spontaneous violence that erupted in London at the height of the assembly movement in Spain, Portugal, and Greece during the summer of 2011. Formally speaking, assembly movements are characterized by opting out of insurrectionary violence, but its ranks nonetheless include many people who have engaged in violent unrest at one time or another. We cannot say that such people have changed their mind or are no longer enraged, for the outrageous conditions of daily violence they suffer have not waned. And as registered by the historical evidence in every assembly-movement situation, including Occupy actions in the United States, the response of established power inevitably turns to violent police repression. So, although the specific structure of assembly-movement demands for direct democracy deserves our closest attention as a form of radical democratic politics, its distance from spontaneous violence out of sheer rage is infinitesimal and always present as a possible turn at any moment.

So the key question becomes: What is the politics of rage? Or even more: Is there a politics of rage? When the answer is yes, the index is almost always some sort of Jacobin imaginary, which certainly makes historical sense. However, the Jacobin imaginary is quintessentially a vanguardist enactment of radical politics, and its huge influence on the history of Marxist politics has no doubt negatively affected the radical democratic capacity of the history of the workers movement—council communism and anarcho-syndicalism. So, while respecting the radical importance of spontaneous modes of insurrection that are expressions of rage and often (though not necessarily) violent, we should remain aware—as was, after all, Rosa Luxemburg herself, the most insightful thinker of spontaneous action—of the danger that such expressions may be hijacked by short-term adventurist militant interests or merely remain enclosed in nihilistic aesthetics of destruction, which can only be antidemocratic. The assembly movement is by definition opposed to any vanguardism, and that is its greatest power. Insofar as it is invested in direct democracy in its multiple manifestations in 2011 (Egypt and Tunisia, Greece and Spain, OWS), the assembly movement has gone quite far to channel a politics of rage toward altering certain ingrained assumptions and social habits, certain unquestioned modes of thought and modes of living. I cannot help but recall here the notion of rage as it was understood in the multiple ancient Greek sense of the word *orgē*, which, at the base of it all, signifies passion, the very power invoked by Sophocles in *Antigone* as one of the formidable (and yet terrifying—*deinon*) capacities of human beings: *astynomous orgas*, the passions that institute and legislate cities, societies. In that sense, *orgē* resides always at the core of the law, and the Sophoclean phrase can be interpreted to point to the constituent power of rage as that (*poiētic*) sentiment of creation/destruction that overturns and overcomes the authority of tacit consent to established power.[6]

6. I owe this quick reflection on the politics of rage to a public conversation with Sophie Klimis at the meeting of *Cahiers Castoriadis* on "L'Autonomie en pratique(s)" in Brussels in May 2011. See also her essay "Antigone et Créon à la lumière du terrifiant/extraordinaire de l'humanité tragique," in *Antigone et la résistance civile*, ed. L. Couloubaritsis and F. Ost (Brussels: Ousia, 2004), 63–102.

Whatever their specific differences, assembly movements are characterized by sheer coming together of people representing themselves, without specific demands tied to political self-interest, except to declare their withdrawal of consent to established power. The logic is simple, which is why it is so brutally real: Established power is in the hands of the very rich who are also very few; against them stand the poor, and they are many. The sheer numbers of the powerless poor constitute a potential power whose actuality is unimaginable by those in control. Unimaginable but not altogether unreal, which is why the rich and few unleash very real police forces against the poor and many daring to protest, lest their numbers grow. Inordinate police repression confirms the movement's political reality inasmuch as it also testifies to the weakness of the liberal state to maintain its persona of legal deliberation and consensus.[7] The movement is real because the problems it addresses are real, and because real people, independent of established political bodies, have decided to confront the inequities of established power on the most tangible reality the public sphere offers. The fact that in the era of virtual social network spaces the street returns to remind us of its concrete public presence is itself a register of the hard reality of this movement.

This is neither to minimize nor to overlook the real power of new social network media and the way they have opened avenues for radically new conceptualizations and actualizations of public space. The concrete role these new technologies have played in all recent instances of assembly movements has been aptly documented. On the other hand, to overplay their significance is not only to fetishize them, thereby playing to the very consumerist imaginary that they presumably resist, but also to underplay the power of actual public assembly. Even if we were to say that the

7. I have addressed this politico-philosophical quandary in "Enlightenment and Paranomia," in *Does Literature Think?* (Stanford, Calif.: Stanford University Press, 2003), 49–89.

urban youth culture with its Facebook and other networking was the core fuel of the Tahrir Square explosion—which is demonstrably not the case, but for the sake of argument—what makes Tahrir Square in 2011 an event of historic magnitude is the actual assembly of real bodies out on the street. No virtual assembly, no matter how sophisticated and inventive, could ever register such a radical event to the point of deposing a regime without firing a gun. The reality of virtual publics hinges on their actualizing real public spaces, as real as they have ever been since the notion of "public" was first created and consciously realized in actual three-dimensional social space, whether this was in ancient Athens or wherever. Radical street politics can still take place without virtual social networks, but radical social network politics cannot take place without the street.

There is an interesting paradox in the name "assembly movement" in the sense that assembly signifies some sort of spatial watershed, a coming or standing together in place, in (public) space. But one does not need to be Aristotelian to underline that movement means change (*alloiosis*)—alteration. As a concept, "movement" bears within itself a certain otherness, a capacity for othering—both of itself and of the space in which it occurs or that it traverses. This is conceptually its democratic essence, if we take seriously the idea that a democratic society would valorize the creation of new determinations—of society, of life, of law, of space, of public, of private. Castoriadis's simple phrase "A society that determines itself otherwise"[8] is a fine description of the social logic of democracy, if we understand "otherwise" to mean a radical alteration of what is already established as instituted self-determination—the specific constitutional state, the specific national culture, and so on—which does not, however, annihilate people's daring to alter

8. Cornelius Castoriadis, *Démocratie et relativisme* (Paris: Mille et Une Nuits, 2010), 54.

self-determined meanings so that something altogether other may emerge.

No doubt, historically we are speaking of a movement that spans a great geopolitical range, even if this expanse is discontinuous. Less an outcome of contagion and more a phenomenon of resonance, a process of people assembling themselves in public spaces starting arguably in Tunisia and Egypt, then in Spain and Greece, and eventually in various cities in the United States, it signifies a broader phenomenon that cannot be called global in the strict sense—because there are parts of the globe that remain still in deep political sleep—but no doubt has global dimensions in the very manifestation of its differential particularity. "Movement," in this respect, refers to this very process of resonance, the way in which otherwise distinct events emerging from their particular social-historical ground come to recognize themselves in one another without evading their particularity.[9] The movement is signified in the actual reverberation of new modes of political being. Concretely, it is signified in the very mobilization of people otherwise unknown and unconnected to one another who come to form a new collective subjectivity through the experience of association, of coming together in a public space. We cannot discount the radical transformative power of this shared experience qua experience. Regardless of the outcome of these movements individually or the assembly-movement phenomenon as a whole, the experiences of those present, of those who have made it happen, is certain to be indelible, to mark a self-transformative moment. The wager consists in what people will make of this indelible experience politically.

———

In the early days of the Egyptian uprising, indeed, just two days after Hosni Mubarak was deposed, I wrote that in the

9. For an insightful articulation of resonance in direct reference to these events, see Gaston Cardillo's "Resonance and the Egyptian Revolution," on the blog Space and Politics, http://spaceandpolitics.blogspot.gr/2011/02/resonance-and-egyptian-revolution.html.

face of the events in Egypt and Tunisia, we saw the very idea of revolutionary action transformed before our eyes while, at the same time, remaining connected to its elemental and integral significance.[10] The Tunisians and the Egyptians showed us that revolutionary action need no longer mean the violent over-throw of a political regime in an orchestrated (or hijacked) ac-tion under the command of a revolutionary vanguard, secular or religious—an action that inevitably leads to some sort of civil war that never ends for the generations who experience it and indelibly marks the generations that follow it. As a result of these people's actions, I argued, revolution now means what it has always meant in essence: the people's withdrawal of their consent to power.

The disclosure here was that in the last instance, no regime can continue to exist without the consent of the society it reigns over, whether this consent is conscious or unconscious, willful or coerced, driven by interest or driven by fear. This is, of course, an old and unfortunately forgotten idea, obscured by revolutionary history since the English Revolution of 1642. We need to recall the great Etienne de La Boétie, who first spoke of voluntary servitude in 1549 (nearly a century earlier), simultaneously directing attention to the fact that the many need only realize they hold more power than the One who nominally controls them. I remind us here of one of his cele-brated arguments:

> Yet there is neither need to combat this single tyrant, nor to defend oneself against him. He is defeated by himself, as long as the coun-try does not consent to its servitude. One need not take anything away from him, so long as one does not give him anything. There is no need for the country to put itself into trouble of doing anything for itself, only that it does not do anything against itself. It is thus the peoples themselves who let themselves, or rather cause themselves

10. See my post on the Immanent Frame, http://blogs.ssrc.org/tif/2011/02 /15/withdrawing-consent/.

to be despoiled, since by ceasing to submit they will rid themselves of their servitude.[11]

Although the figure of power in this Renaissance text is monarchical, La Boétie's calling remains perfectly apt in the contemporary situation, where the world's ubiquitous oligarchies, including those who trade in the name of democracy, sustain themselves with the profound collaboration of a *dēmos* that disavows its responsibility for self-determination and self-governance. Perhaps this is because, to the degree they operate behind a national state apparatus, these oligarchies are still configured in terms of singular power, of an *archē* that is its own *telos*, in which the people are complicit until they withdraw their consent.

Much can be learned from how the events in Tunisia and Egypt were conducted in 2011 and, even though they are not quite the same, from the unfolding events in the rest of the Arab world, even where matters degenerated into the rote violence of civil war, as in Libya or Syria. In Egypt, at this point, although no one can predict the ultimate outcome—for the presidential elections are by no means the outcome but just a phase in a process no serious person can claim to foretell—daily life on the ground shows demonstrable signs of irreversible change, not only in the complex processes of figuring out the strains of democratic institution but also in the broad presence of new forms of popular expression and imagination, a

---

11. Etienne de la Boétie, "On Voluntary Servitude," in *Freedom over Servitude: Montaigne, La Boétie and* On Voluntary Servitude, ed. and trans. David Lewis Schaefer (Westport, Conn.: Greenwood Press, 1998), 194. The French quotation is as follows: "Or ce tyran seul, il n'est pas besoin de le combattre, ni de l'abattre. Il est défait de lui-même, pourvu que le pays ne consente point à sa servitude. Il ne s'agit pas de lui ôter quelque chose, mais de ne rien lui donner. Pas besoin que le pays se mette en peine de faire rien pour soi, pourvu qu'il ne fasse rien contre soi. Ce sont donc les peuples eux-mêmes qui se laissent, ou plutôt qui se font malmener, puisqu'ils en seraient quittes en cessant de servir."

kind of street theatricality and public improvisational musical poetics that are unprecedented in Egyptian society.[12] The inevitable contention between these new modes of public expression and demands, coming from Salafi quarters, for a more traditional Muslim attitude in public is what the risk of democracy entails.

Whoever considers the current conditions of antagonism a setback romanticizes the insurrectionary moment as if it is indeed a moment and the revolutionary trajectory as if indeed it means a progressive linearity. Surely, it is impossible to sustain the orchestrated synergy of the differential constituencies that during eighteen days of explosive popular action in January 2011 interwove a technologically ingenious urban youth; a deeply entrenched and experienced workers syndicalist movement; the initiative of independent women in and out of the family structure, some devout, some secular; the liberal bourgeoisie of the main Egyptian cities; the well-trained organization of the Muslim Brotherhood in the professional classes; and above all, the spontaneously and autonomously enraged association of tens of thousands of the poorest of the poor. The sense from people on the ground—and I can speak only secondhand—is that the people, though patient with the difficulty of forging new institutions, will tolerate no setback, for they have seen what autonomous action looks like and have understood what it can come to mean. The first step from being governed to governing oneself is for the people to overcome

12. Of the voluminous work coming to print with lightning speed, see Elliot Colla, "The Poetry of Revolt," originally posted on *Al Jadaliyya* and reprinted in *The Dawn of Arab Uprisings: End of an Old Order?*, ed. Bassam Haddad, Rosie Bsheer, and Ziad Abu-Rish (London: Pluto Press, 2012); Samia Mehrez, ed., *Translating Egypt's Revolution* (Cairo: American University in Cairo Press, 2012); and Ashraf Khalil, *Liberation Square: Inside the Egyptian Revolution and the Birth of a Nation* (New York: St. Martins Press, 2012). For the situation in Tunisia, with all kinds of reflections on Egypt, see the unique collection "Tunisia Dossier: The Tunisian Revolution of Dignity," ed. Ronald Judy, *boundary 2* 39, no. 1 (Winter 2012).

their fear of government—that is, not only literally the fear of repression by the government but also the fear of assuming responsibility for government entirely on their own. The turn to violent resistance against the army, which we have seen on a couple of occasions since the events at Tahrir Square, as well as the resistance to governing Muslim Brotherhood's alliance with neoliberalism subsequently, is precisely the manifestation of this newly gained fearlessness.

We cannot prophesy an outcome in history, but we can judge a situation enough to know when there is no turning back. And that is precisely what is revolutionary about this occasion. The outcome may end up being worse, or it may end up being inconceivably other, but there is no way for things to return to where they were. The Egyptian people have changed the course of their history and, even more, have left an unerasable mark on the history of Arab societies. This carries a signification of its own, regardless of the trajectory of Egyptian institutional politics, as we speak or in the future.[13] The barrage of arguments in Western media about the subsequent Islamization of the revolution cannot do anything to hide their Orientalist predisposition. However, if we consider that the matter has been settled with the Muslim Brotherhood's assumption of the helm of institutional governance, as if indeed this was the glorious purpose of the Arab Spring, then we will be confined in precisely this same Orientalist trap, even if from the other side. Such positions could be celebrating the current regime as the "moderate" Erdoğan style of Islamic governance

13. I still hold to this position, even if Egyptian president Mohamed Morsi has decreed virtually monarchical power by putting himself above the law in the name of "protecting the Revolution." It is worth noting the significant resistance from various quarters of Egyptian society, despite the bleakness of this typical reversal. The time frame of how revolutionary power degenerates to monarchical power can never be generalized or predicted, but one thing is certain: if a people have overthrown a monarch, surely the same people can overthrow another, even one who has usurped their name.

that is to serve as the antidote to the model of the Iranian Revolution. But they would be guilty of a double self-denial of the facts that (1) Erdoğan's Turkey is the epitome of yet another corrupt autocratic state, where the prescription of an alleged Islamic ethics against nationalist secularism is the means of an extraordinary drive for mass pacification and capitulation (which the capitalist West finds all too convenient); and (2) the antidote to the model of the Iranian Revolution is not the election of Mohamed Morsi, but precisely the image of the assembly of all kinds of disparate segments of Egyptian society in Tahrir Square, secular and religious, Muslim and Coptic, young and old, men and women, urban bourgeois and provincial working classes, which made this a glorious secular event.

The explosive response of masses of Muslims in Egypt and elsewhere in September 2012 as a result of the outrageous provocation of the Internet film denigrating the Prophet took place precisely in the domain opened by the Arab Spring as a secular event. This is the case even if the overtly monolithic religious tenets of the protests efface the differential field of the revolution, even with unprecedented acts of destruction (such as the pillaging and torching of the American School in Tunis, which had been left unharmed in the initial uprising). The bitter lesson of these protests is that the resistance of disenfranchised peoples in Muslim societies—or just as well, Muslim immigrant workers in European societies—is being restricted to a response coded (and unfortunately accepted) as "religious"; the rampant Islamophobia of the West is, alas, an endless resource of this theologization of political resistance to global capital. In this light, the newly instituted openness of the Arab Spring movements carries an ever-greater risk, but after all, the epistemological ground of the secular is certainly not security. In the last instance, secular epistemology rests on worldly self-determination, and the content of this "self" cannot be prescribed, bounded, or secured a priori by an ideological command, whether this command is secular or religious.

I understand why my proposition that the Egyptian events presented the world with a revolutionary condition was confronted with suspicion, even before the recent denouement. It is interesting to note that this suspicion came essentially from two opposite quarters. For one, my assessment of the Egyptian uprising as an innovation in the history of revolution, and in this respect a secular event, was criticized in various antisecularist circles in the American academy as an attempt to hijack the events for the benefit of a Western politico-philosophical canon. This is absurd on too many fronts to recount (already since the revolution in Haiti in 1803, revolutionary history has exceeded the West), but most befuddling is the inability of those positions to recognize their own self-Orientalization in their insistence that the spontaneous insurrectionary action of Egyptians of all classes and creeds cannot be "Western" in any shape or form and under any circumstances. Even if all societies around the world espoused democratic values tomorrow, they would hardly become "Westernized" as a result—it seems utterly banal to point this out. The knee-jerk fear of the "Western" in unqualified terms is mind-boggling when we are engaged in serious analysis. On the other hand, the Eurocentric dismissal that there is nothing new in the events as they are unfolding is equally Orientalist and even "nativist" in an utterly perverse way—although I don't need to elaborate why. So is the self-assured cynicism that speaks of a mere two-week affair that cannot possibly have anything to do with revolution. The persistent phantasm of protracted multiyear civil strife as the conventional paradigm of a revolutionary situation says a lot about the intransigent privilege of the debilitated social imaginary that governs much of so-called Western thinking nowadays.

As does the phantasm of the revolutionary moment and the obsession with the singularity of the event. Post Tahrir, the resurgence of the people's demands for real democracy in Egypt, after a series of setbacks to military bureaucratic ways—but also the presidential election itself, all the more because it is being offered as an indication of institutional stability that seals the proceedings once and for all—demonstrates that the temporality of radical events is never indeed momentary. This is ultimately a Leninist notion, even in Alain Badiou's mind. Even the most catastrophic event might be said to unleash the power of the time that enabled it. Even as it creates its own time, no event can fully escape the time that permeates it. Only in the fantasy space of the psyche can we speak of events (or anything, for that matter) existing without temporality. Not so in history. The desire, of course, to perform the non-temporality of the dream state in history is understandable, but it is just that: a desire. Even the imagined future, within a historical frame, is riveted by time—real time, even if not yet realized.

Likewise, an event that creates a rupture in time is riveted by multiplicity, interruptibility, heterochronicity, reiteration, and, in the end, reinstitution. The most important element of the Greek demand for "immediate democracy" in the Syntagma Square assembly in the summer of 2011 is precisely the symbolic explosion of this immediacy as it comes to be mediated by the effect of its own occurrence, much as radiation permeates and displaces the explosion of the bomb that unleashes it. Even while brimming with rage or indignation, even when only what is immediate has retained a modicum of meaning in the course of an otherwise meaningless life, one must learn to remain patient, persistent, and ever more inventive in one's commitment to irreversible transformation that is inevitably long lasting even if it is sensible in a microsecond.

The events of the Arab Spring were crucial catalysts of the movements in Spain and Greece in the spring and summer of 2011, as the so-called PIIGS crisis in Europe went into full swing and Greece entered its resolute conditions of bankruptcy. In some ways, the effect unleashed by the insurgent social imaginary in Tahrir Square on the Syntagma Square assembly movement can be seen as a palindrome formation if one thinks of how the Athens insurgency in December 2008 influenced the radicalization of youth in various parts of the Arab world.[14]

The Greek situation, starting in December 2008 and still unfolding, may have come to signify the most dramatic articulation of the battlefield between democracy and capitalism, which is more than ever, I repeat, the essential political problem of our times.[15] In 2012 we witnessed the extraordinary contradiction of national elections in Greece being conducted in the midst of an unprecedented collapse of credibility of the entire political system. A bankrupt country whose population was profoundly disaffected with the entire political system gathered to exercise its democratic right to elect officials that were to preside over a national terrain that had effectively lost its sovereignty. What does this mean? Although the nation-state still remains the requisite form of society's self-determination, the pillar of integrity of the nation form since the advent of modernity—namely, the national economy—has been thoroughly dismantled by the dynamics of a globalized economy that couldn't care less about national boundaries, cultural particularities, social histories, or, even more, societies themselves as self-recognized collectives of real men and women whose very conditions of life are at stake.

14. See A. G Schwarz, Tasos Sagris, and the Void Network, *We Are an Image of the Future: The Greek Revolts of December 2008* (Oakland, Calif.: AK Press, 2010); Andreas Kalyvas, "An Anomaly? Some Reflections on the Greek December 2008," *Constellations* 17, no. 2 (2010): 351–65; and Neni Panourgia, "Stones (Papers, Humans)," *Journal of Modern Greek Studies* 28, no. 2 (October 2010): 199–224.

15. In addition to Athena Athanasiou's book *The Crisis as "State of Exception"* mentioned earlier, the other equally insightful and passionate account of the Greek crisis—from the December events of 2008 to the assembly movement of summer 2011 and to current political resistance to the asphyxiating austerity measures—is given by Costas Douzinas in a consistent array of opinion pieces in the *Guardian* and elsewhere, collected and culminating in his book *Resistance and Philosophy during the Crisis* (Athens: Alexandria, 2012).

This is not meant to be taken metaphorically. Greeks are literally perishing in order to satisfy ruthless profit margins of global financial capital. Suicide numbers have skyrocketed (estimated at nearly three thousand in two years' time) in a country that statistically had the lowest suicide rate in the world. Suicides have now become a daily occurrence, a bona fide social phenomenon in a society that may be characterized in all kinds of ways but neither by its violence nor its depressive behavior. Many more than those who choose to take their own lives so as not to saddle their kin with insurmountable debt are living in borderline hunger conditions, a level of poverty not seen since World War II and its aftermath. Moreover, these conditions have been created with unprecedented speed—a kind of flash impoverishment on a mass scale, which can happen only when all terms of a national economy are annihilated and external financial forces wield direct political power over a national terrain. This is why, although Greece still exists on the map of nations under a sovereign flag, it is effectively a country on hold—or under hold, a country whose sovereignty has been mortgaged.[16]

16. That Greek society itself is culpable for this condition by having fallen enthusiastically into the trap of stupid consumerism enabled by easy money flowing in from the banks of Europe and global speculative capital looking for quick and easy profits, while it has been simultaneously supported by the historical accident of an enormous influx of cheap immigrant labor from collapsed former Soviet societies and then from waves of refugees from wars and poverty in the Middle East, South Asia, and Africa who saw Greece as the gateway to the European Union, does not absolve the elites of global capital and the European Union specifically of the criminal act of staging an onslaught to wipe out a whole way of life—an intrinsically anticapitalist way of life—that arguably goes back centuries. Yes, the Greeks themselves went against this precious way of life, and I have been criticizing Greek excesses and irresponsibilities for years, even before *Dream Nation* (1996). But now is the time to combat both the subjugation of the Greek people and the unabashed Orientalization that escorts it from societies no less corrupt, no less capitulating to reckless consumerism, and no less complicit in the chase for greed and profit, whatever may be their myths of cultural morality and national purity.

The social effects of these conditions have been devastating. It is often said that the German government under Chancellor Angela Merkel spearheaded this brutal austerity program because it was haunted by its Weimar past: hyperinflation, impoverishment, social capitulation, political malaise, and the rise of fascism. What seems to have escaped the pundits who trade in such clichés is that German policies are producing new Weimars elsewhere in Europe; Weimar conditions are the hottest export commodity in neoliberal economics. All aspects of the Greek situation corroborate this fact. The increasing public presence and new parliamentary status of Golden Dawn is no accident. This neo-Nazi fringe group of thugs and bona fide criminals has been exploiting the surge of nationalist sentiment that emerged as a kind of defensive knee-jerk reaction of a people who suddenly have to endure not only conditions of flash impoverishment but also an onslaught of Orientalist attacks on its character and its history by the mainstream press in Germany, Britain, and even the United States. But, as is commonly known in Europe, this is a typical situation, hardly particular to Greeks. Coupled with the collapse of the credibility of the entire political system, a resurgent defensive nationalism does render society vulnerable to fascist expression. However, that said, in the end this new fascist phenomenon of Golden Dawn is Greece's internal story and the responsibility of its own society. Golden Dawn gains points in the ranks of those driven by nationalist and (literally) reactionary sentiment with acts of bogus philanthropy, while it actively supports the entire neoliberal agenda of big capital. The notorious charge of Greeks not living up to their taxation responsibilities—in terms of how tax evasion hurts the financial capacity of public welfare—is more applicable at the level of the richest and greediest conglomerates of industrialists, media, and crony politicians. Although the fascist Golden Dawn claims to be against these conglomerates, in reality it acts in their service; its national-populist rhetoric is nothing but a smokescreen, In the end, the struggle against global capital in Greece will be fought on the same terrain as the struggle against this front of fascist thugs, against the resurgent nationalism of parts of the population (in the full biopolitical range that implicates not just race, but also the full gamut of gender and sexuality politics), and against any tendency to regard the enormous problem of immigration and undocumented labor (now nearly 20 percent of the population) as a social and historical problem, not a mere humanitarian or human rights problem, as has unfortunately been the tendency in much of the radical Left.

Any reasonable assessment of this abhorrent situation would have to confront the fact that Greece exemplifies the terrain of a specific experiment: How far can the commands of a globalized economy push against a specific society's endurance or will? From the perspective of global capital, Greece is a low-risk entity if the experiment fails. It is a small economy, globally inconsequential, and hence of limited liability from a strictly economic standpoint. The political stakes, however, bear unprecedented consequences. As the institutions of the European Union are failing and national sovereignty is waning, the only option for European peoples to protect their future is to mobilize broad and defiant democratic movements that will regain control of the political terrain from global market forces. The experiment cuts both ways, and as rebelling youth all over the globe explicitly acknowledge, Greece is currently at the forefront of this battle. Winning this battle stands to benefit not just Greeks but also the broader demands of European peoples, who find themselves on the brink of similar dismantling of their sovereignty by global capital, which has turned European political leaders into mere stooges.

This is why what is happening to Greece is not merely an economic experiment. Chancellor Merkel has been quoted as admitting that in imposing such painful austerity measures, the troika (the European Commission, the European Central Bank, and the International Monetary Fund) singled out Greece for punishment as a lesson to any other European societies that might consider resisting its commands.[17] Nothing is surprising here, least of all the cynicism of both global financial power and the mainstream media in its service. It is, in many ways, an old story. This is not the first time in history where the fate of whole societies is held in the hands of bankers, although it is our duty to remember that when this is pushed to the extreme, societies unravel in extraordinary violence and international war. Given that the European Union as a political ideal was constituted in order to prevent such unraveling, it is remarkable that its political and economic leadership is most responsible for pursuing this catastrophic course against all sense of prudence and measure.

Greece is a small country and a small economy. It is, therefore, convenient ground for an experiment of punitive neoliberal commands, with negligible economic liability. What about the stakes of the political? Or is the political is no longer a factor, now that global economic factors are themselves acting politically? History is surely ahead of us and obeys no providence. But whichever way it plays out, as we now stand, Greek resistance to becoming such an experiment has vast consequences because it pertains to the future of all Europe. If Greece goes down and is successfully shackled by the commands of global capital, there will have emerged within the ranks of the European Union a precedent that dismantles its sovereignty as a political project. However it is to happen, whether by total capitulation or by expulsion, to kill Greece is for the European Union to commit suicide. And it may be that global financial interests don't care (they are indeed, to judge by recent events, entirely careless), but shouldn't real populations care about who and what determines their future, especially when their future

17. Marcus Walker, "How a Radical Greek Rescue Plan Fell Short," *Wall Street Journal*, May 19, 2012, http://online.wsj.com/article/SB10001424052702 30420360457739396419865 2568.html?mod=googlenews_wsj.

seems endangered? We have returned to the quandary I posed at the outset.

The recent phenomenon of assembly movements in occupied public spaces, whatever their shortcomings, suggests that in the wake of the crisis in the centers of financial capitalism, people may be emerging from their consumerist stupor to realize that their relative prosperity is entirely manufactured outside their domain of control (even outside the domain of their desire, but that is another conversation) and so can be—with unfathomable speed and on an unprecedented scale—almost instantly revoked. This painful awakening would include the realization that state mechanisms have become thoroughly compromised as ruling elites have come to trade their country's sovereignty for a small piece of the financial pie. Much can be learned in this regard from Nadia Urbinati's argument that we are undergoing "an epochal mutation" whereby the historic compromise, since the market crash of 1929, between capitalist elites and middle-class civil society interests (including the mechanisms of representative government in the service of social welfare) has come to an irreversible end.[18] In effect, to follow Urbinati's argument, this was none other than a compromise between capitalism and liberal democracy, strictly speaking, whereby a minimum circulation of surplus wealth (to link here with the analysis by Varoufakis cited at the outset) would ensure the civil security of commodity consumers. The demise of the social welfare state, which incidentally coincides with the demise of the national economy as society's primary mechanism of wealth production, is signified by virtue of what amounts to a class secession as the capitalist elite abandons its alliance—or, what is in effect the same thing, colonizes its class political apparatus (established, one might say, since the revolutionary

18. Nadia Urbinati, "La rinascita della politica," http://www.italianieuropei .it/it/italianieuropei-4-2012/item/2588-la-rinascita-della-politica/2588-la -rinascita-della-politica.html.

era)—by governing, with minimal mediation, from the position of the global market as such.

The challenge, Urbinati argues in like spirit to my argument here, is a turn to a new political imaginary or, perhaps more accurately, the reawakening of the political toward its elemental aspects: mass citizen action, first of all out in the streets, as this becomes the only available uncompromised option, but then also at the ballot box, the routine of which is reconfigured as citizens revoke their consent to the very clientelist relations they had helped foster. In this sense, the electoral field itself emerges as a new terrain of mass citizen action, a new public space of struggle, because the perfunctory electoral habitus of somnambulant clients of political and ideological machines is disrupted by the experience of street politics. In this sense, the democratic institution of elections is taken out of the signifying framework of liberalism and opened up to all kinds of radical traditions in the historical trajectory of democratic practices. Given the deregulation of the political and the consequent financial takeover of the field of government, the first gesture of reclaiming the political is to take over—to occupy—public spaces in mass numbers, including the public space of elections.[19] We have reached a point when the very language of numbers that discredits the existence of the social individual can be countered only by large numbers of real individuals

---

19. Again, I do not want to minimize the political importance of new technologies and social media networks. The work of Anonymous or WikiLeaks, for example, is at the forefront of new modes of struggle against established power—and this is the very least one can expect if we consider that on the other side, war is conducted by unmanned drone aircraft on such an unprecedented scale that, as journalist Michael Hastings quipped, "never have so few killed so many by remote control." (See "The Drone Wars," *Rolling Stone* 1155 [April 26, 2012]: 42.) But these new technological capacities for social organization make the mass presence of people coming together in the street to fight with their actual bodies all the more remarkable and, as the dire police measures taken by the liberal state indicate, all the more real.

who demand back their abrogated self-determination against capitulation to the language of numbers.

In the era of globalized deterritorialization by the faceless politics of finance, we observe the most elemental politics of all: the politics of actual people producing a new democratic public that reclaims society's territory. This is not about returning to old models, defending some ancestral notion of the nation, some sort of autochthony. It is about reestablishing the territory of self-determination, the essential ground for any real democracy. The increasing phenomenon of fanatic nationalism (even fascism) in Europe is just as much a consequence of the debilitating deterritorialization of globalized economy, so it must be combated with equal force and determination, for it trades one mode of capitulation (economic) for another (ideological). In this sense, radical democratic movements are facing a double task: redrawing the boundaries of self-determination of specific societies and yet, at the same time, redrawing the capacity for a new international, that is, forging a solidarity among peoples in different societies who come together precisely in their *co-incidence* of resistance to globalized incapacitation.

I understand why many people would say with the best intentions that this analysis is at the very least premature, and that what has taken place will not go beyond "the year of dreaming dangerously," as Slavoj Žižek has cleverly named the experiences of 2011 in his recent book.[20] For one thing, the explosion of radical democratic movements has been happening in a specific geography of the global economic sphere; we can speak neither of a global crisis of capitalism—no matter how chain-linked are all aspects of capital—nor of a global movement against capitalism. Moreover, many people doubt that radical changes can be effected at all, even by those constituencies who have erupted against the politics of global capital with such intensity; they point out that mere withdrawal of consent to

20. Slavoj Žižek, *The Year of Dreaming Dangerously* (London: Verso, 2012).

established power is inadequate without the move to constitu-ent power. Strictly speaking, such critiques are right: With-drawal of consent to heteronomous power (a negative action) must be followed by constituent action of autonomous power (a positive action) for democracy to be fully enacted as a regime (*kratos*). However, without the first, nothing happens at all. And, indeed, the first moment—withdrawal of consent to power—is in itself, in its negativity, autonomous action. This is the profound lesson of La Boétie's discourse, a lesson regretta-bly not learned.

Of course, withdrawal of consent to power always takes place in specific contingencies, specific social-historical param-eters. One would be hard pressed to expect or demand that *sans-papiers* or stateless persons be encumbered with the duty to withdraw their consent. What consent? Only those who con-stitute the realm of the governed can be called on to withdraw consent—called on by historical conditions, because it is a self-determined calling that they are enacting. The disenfranchised are not, strictly speaking, ruled; they are considered ungovern-able and are situated outside rule, outside both the parameters of the nation-state and the rule of law. Their consent is not asked for, nor do they give it, even if they presumably cared to do so, because they simply have no access to power. They are disenfranchised precisely so as not to have any access to the dynamics of rule; hence they can be oppressed with impunity. (This is not to say that the disenfranchised should be consid-ered deprived of dissenting capacities; it is to say that in their case dissent can be only outright rebellion.) This situation is especially true in European societies, where vast masses of im-migrant peoples, directly and existentially affected by the po-litical takeover of global capital, continue to be excluded from the boundaries of civil law and thereby from the capacity to enlist or withdraw their consent on how these boundaries may be established, maintained, and enforced. I do not mean here to suggest that citizenship is the a priori condition for democ-racy; strictly speaking, this is a nonsensical proposition, and in any case it places citizenship in a heteronomous relation to democracy. Democracy entails citizenship as a terrain of conquest, as political power to be won for all participants equally, not as a transcendental principle to be followed or enacted as a command. Indeed, what happens in situations where mass withdrawal of consent takes place is a broadening of the range of those who get access to power, who become powerful, and therefore can move to a position of interrogation and alteration of what exists. Hence the importance of constituent power all the more: A revolutionary situation occurs precisely when, as a direct effect of those who withdraw their consent, a different constituent power emerges, and the relation between ruler and ruled, governing and governed, is transformed. Here I agree with Antonio Negri's antifoundational sense of constituent power that pits it very much against both theological power and sovereignty as such (whose theological trappings in modern societies have not yet been overcome anyway). The problematic of constituent power makes sense only in a democratic situation, where sovereignty never takes precedence over the political constitution of the people's power, power in its becoming power.[21]

This means as well that whatever political forces understand themselves as part of the Left also have to alter their historical relation to the understanding of constituent power and governmentality. It was interesting and encouraging to see in Greece that ranks of SYRIZA (Coalition of the Radical Left), during the 2012 electoral campaign, were organizing open and public discussions on the question "What is a government of the Left?" in a fashion similar to open discussions that took place in Syntagma Square during the peak of the assembly movement in June 2011. In emerging as a real government option in the Greek elections of 2012 and subsequently leading the polls for

---

21. Among many writings on this issue, see especially Antonio Negri, *Insurgencies: Constituent Power and the Modern State*, trans. Maurizia Boscagli (Minneapolis: University of Minnesota Press, 1999), 1–36.

the next projected elections, SYRIZA faces the taking on of enormous responsibility to the Greek public, the first step of which would be to overcome the Left's general taboo on governance. Outside revolutionary situations—indeed, because of its revolutionary legacy—the Left worldwide has thrived in the role of mere opposition to ruling parties in parliamentary democracies. One might say that the Left's attachment to opposition has traditionally been so great that any discourse about its taking on the responsibility of government was automatically considered a compromise or even a betrayal of principles. That this attitude weakened over time the political capacity of the Left to express the popular will has not been given proper attention among its ranks, including its intellectuals.[22] So, in concrete terms, the very first responsibility of SYRIZA, were it to be elected to power, would be to annul the void of proper policing of social justice. Greek society is currently undergoing unprecedented levels of anomie and lawlessness across the board, including, of course, the ranks of the police itself, which is rife with fascist elements. The whole matter is characterized by unheard-of levels of street violence and criminality. A governmentality of the Left would have to come to terms with what it means to execute proper legal justice against all elements of society who criminally benefit themselves to the detriment of others. This cannot be conducted merely by repealing unjust laws; it would require enforcing existing laws that are upheld as essential to democratic freedoms. What is now at stake for Greek society is whether its future will be a democratic polity of social justice or a jungle of limitless Mafia tactics. That's the bottom line.

22. A notable exception is Slavoj Žižek in many of his recent political texts. In addition to arguments in much of *The Year of Dreaming Dangerously*, one text that resonates with my positions here (although I would still question his attachment to the language of permanent state of exception) is his article "A Permanent Economic Emergency," *New Left Review* 64 (July–August 2010), http://newleftreview.org/II/64/slavoj-zizek-a-permanent-economic-emergency.

If, as Ariella Azoulay has argued, the recent wave of "civil revolution"—her term for the assembly-movement phenomenon, including the Arab Spring—has rewritten the syntax of revolution,[23] then we might add that it has rewritten the (revolutionary) exigency to govern, not by abolishing the law, but by altering the law to abolish relentless financial anomie and social injustice. The old clichéd dilemma "Revolution or Reform?" is utterly inadequate at this stage. Or rather, our present historical conditions are exposing the fact that it has always been inadequate, in fact, nonsensical. For no change in history, even the most immense revolutionary change, annihilates the existing historical field. It just transforms it, which indeed may happen by the creation of new and unprecedented forms. Hence we can speak only of a radical transformation of society, which, cognitively speaking, includes the notion of reform at an elemental level, but insofar as it is radical, it exceeds just a reformation—a rearrangement or reorchestration of existing forms, an adjustment or variation—and necessitates a creation of not merely different but altogether other forms.

Today's assembly movements and demands for immediate democracy are tangible demonstrations of people's profound democratic desire to alter the forms of their social existence, not only in what they stand for but also in how they stand—literally, in that people stand together, united by their condition, demanding what seems impossible: the alteration of an entire system of conducting politics and economics, government and legislation, law and justice. What is consistently remarkable in all assembly-movement occasions, regardless of social-historical specifics, is that people come to realize that together they learn new ways of what it means to be a citizen, what it means to be free, what it means to stand together with another person you don't otherwise know. What it means to

23. Ariella Azoulay, "Revolution," in *Political Concepts: A Critical Lexicon* 2 (Winter 2012), http://www.discoursenotebook.org/politicalconcepts/revolution-ariella-azoulay/.

act together, even if the goal is yet unclear, even if the demand is noninstrumental.

At the same time, assembly movements have shown themselves to be extraordinary schools in the making, where people educate themselves on how to move democracy beyond the perfunctory electoral ritual. Elections may signal democracy's essence but are degraded and incapacitated when elected representatives are bought and driven by the economic interests of the powerful few. The assembly movement casts a different light on the electoral institution—Greece being a case in point, but also the 2012 U.S. presidential election, which was no doubt affected by the spirit and the language of OWS, even if the victorious Democratic Party is in essence adversarial to the movement. Regardless of specific outcomes, of internal setbacks or successful repressions, of being fatigued or outwitted, the assembly-movement phenomenon cannot be withdrawn from the sphere of contemporary politics, whether conventional liberal politics or radical democratic politics. The experiences of those present, of those who make it happen, have become indelible; the tangible stuff of the political now appears entirely different to them. Whatever happens to what started as Los Indignados or Occupy Wall Street, the mode of protesting citizens occupying public spaces will persist as long as the system continues its unsustainable ways. Surely, Wall Street will never again bear the same name; its name has been occupied by meanings that subvert its logic. Its symbolic content has been invaded, and in the occupation of its name a new political reality is now potentially open, even if the trajectory against inculcated social practices appears Sisyphean, even if the outcome remains unknown.

Index

Abbas, Sadia, 74
Adams, Suzi, 94, 103n
Adorno, Theodor W., 36, 92, 93n
Aeschylus, 71, 106
Agamben, Giorgio, 82
Allen, Woody, 74
Alteration, 8, 20, 24–25, 44, 61, 97,
    101, 113, 115–16, 152, 157, 159,
    177–79
Anaximander, 104, 106–7, 112, 115
Anidjar, Gil, 32
Anti-secularism, 29, 31–33, 46–47,
    52, 166
Apter, Emily, 1
Arab Spring, 90, 147, 154, 156–57,
    159–67, 179
Aristotle, 21, 25–27, 55–57, 79, 84,
    99, 102, 159
Asad, Talal, 13, 15, 18–23, 25, 31, 46,
    52n, 53, 65
Assembly movements, xix, 143–47,
    154–60, 163, 165, 167–68, 173–75,
    177, 179–80; and *Occupy Wall*

Street, 143, 145–47, 154, 156–57,
    160, 180
Athanasiou, Athena, 151n, 168n
Atheism, 65, 68–69, 72–78, 88–89
Aulagnier, Piera, 125
Autonomy, xviii, 18, 34, 38, 44–45,
    50, 56n, 90–92, 95–96, 99, 103,
    105–8, 110, 115–17, 136, 144,
    163, 176
Autopoiesis, 95–103
Azoulay, Ariella, 179

Bachelard, Gaston, 112
Badiou, Alain, 82, 167
Baltas, Aristides, 75n
Barthes, Roland, xi–xv, xx
Beckett, Samuel, 78
Belief, 42, 49, 61, 68–75, 78–79, 83
Benjamin, Walter, 49, 78
Bennett, Jane, 24
Bergson, Henri, 11
Blasphemy, 52–54
Blumenberg, Hans, 37

Boltanski, Luc, 20n
Bové, Paul, 15n
Brecht, Bertolt, xiii, 153
Breckman, Warren, 121n
Brown, Wendy, 31, 52n
Burke, Edmund, 87
Bush, George W., 33n, 80–81, 145
Butler, Judith, 15–16, 21n, 52n,
     53, 60

Capital, xix, 149, 153, 165, 169–72,
     175–76; and capitalism, xviii–xx,
     40, 93, 132, 146–50, 153–55, 165,
     168, 173, 175; and consumerism,
     xix, 93, 132, 145–46, 149–50, 153,
     158, 169n, 173; and modernity, 9,
     147; and pre-capitalism, 9; and
     regulation, xix, 147–50
Cardillo, Gaston, 160n
Castoriadis, Cornelius, 40, 44, 59,
     71n, 90–119, 122, 123n, 131, 133n,
     134, 159; and the *ensidic*, 100, 102,
     106, 109–10, 113–14, 117; and
     magmas, 102, 104n, 108–14; and
     ontology, 102–3, 105, 133n; and
     the sciences, 95, 100–101, 110,
     112, 115; and *Socialisme ou
     Barbarie*, 94, 122
Christianity, 8, 18–19, 22–23, 29–34,
     36, 37n, 38–42, 47, 49, 57, 63, 65,
     67–73, 79–82, 84, 121, 139–40; in
     America, 14, 33, 46
Citizen, 126n, 131, 152, 174, 179–80
Citizenship, 126n, 152, 176–77
Comparative literature, xvii, 1–7, 11
Connolly, William, 61
Consent to power, xix, 45, 93, 132,
     134, 153, 157, 161, 162n;
     withdrawal of, xviii, 132, 144,
     158, 161–62, 174–77, 180
Constant, Benjamin, 147
Constituent power, 11, 72, 157–58,
     176–77

Constitution, xx, 4, 21, 67, 77, 83,
     95, 97, 99, 103, 115–16, 118, 119,
     127, 128, 131–32, 134, 136, 159, 172
Cosmological abyss, 77–78, 84–85,
     103, 107–8, 117–19, 133n, 136, 142
Creation, 8–9, 20, 25, 26–27, 92, 96,
     99, 101–3, 106–7, 109–13, 117–19,
     122, 124–25, 133, 157, 159, 179
Critique, xvii, 3, 15–25, 28, 32, 35,
     39, 45–46, 54–55, 56n, 58, 60–62,
     127–28
Cultural studies, 5n

Dawkins, Richard, 68, 76
De Certeau, Michel, 70, 72
Decision, 15–21, 24–25, 42, 60–61,
     78, 82–84, 86–87, 116, 148, 150
Democracy, xv, 120–21, 123n,
     126–28, 130–34, 136–44, 147,
     150–52, 159, 162–63, 168, 174–80;
     ancient, 16–18, 95, 112, 116,
     142–43; radical, xvii, xix–xx, 61,
     91–92, 99, 116, 127, 131, 143–44,
     146, 155–57, 159–60, 167, 175,
     179–80; and totalitarianism, 98,
     120, 126, 134–35, 139, 155; and
     violence, xix, 92, 47, 131, 137,
     154, 156–58, 161–62, 164, 167,
     174n, 178
Derrida, Jacques, 18
Descartes, René, 23, 24, 34–35, 58
Destruction, xix, 8, 25, 39, 76–77,
     102–3, 140, 157, 165, 167
Dialectic, xiii, 17, 25, 33, 40, 51,
     78, 93n
Douzinas, Costas, 168n
During, Simon, 31

Enlightenment, 22, 25, 33, 142
Epistemology, xiii, 1, 3–6, 8, 12,
     18n, 25, 35–36, 39–40, 42, 48,
     50, 63, 68, 81, 91, 108, 112, 120,
     139, 165

Eros, 9, 42–43
Ethics, 8, 16, 19–20, 23, 35, 51, 56n, 57, 59, 61, 70, 84, 87, 118, 140, 165

Fanon, Frantz, 52
Fascism, xiii, 38n, 170–71, 175, 178
Finitude, 34, 41, 62, 67, 73, 102–5, 122
Flynn, Bernard, 132n, 134, 135n
Foucault, Michel, xx, 18, 21n, 61, 112
Freud, Sigmund, 39, 41

Gauchet, Marcel, 36, 65
Globalization, xviii, 4, 148, 152, 165, 168–72, 175–76
Greece, xviii–xix, 147, 151n, 152, 154, 156–57, 167–72, 177–78, 180; and December 2008 uprising, xviii–xix, xxvii, 156, 160, 168; and *Golden Dawn*, 170
Greek thought, 7–9, 15–18, 25–27, 37n, 56n, 57, 70–72, 79–80, 82, 102–5, 112, 157
Greenspan, Alan, 149–50

Harris, Sam, 68, 76
Hegel, G.W.F., 10, 33
Heidegger, Martin, 10, 82, 133n
Hellenism, 8, 23
Hesiod, 112
Hessel, Stéphane, 155
Heteronomy, xiv, 14, 28, 35, 43, 45–47, 50, 59–60, 64, 82, 90–94, 98, 101–2, 105–8, 110, 115, 116n, 117–19, 121, 129, 131, 134, 176–77
History, 10–11, 17, 24, 29, 34, 39, 49, 62–63, 66–67, 88, 111–12, 121–22, 125, 129, 138, 142, 164, 167, 172, 179
Hitchens, Christopher, 76
Hobbes, Thomas, 137
Homer, 7, 38n, 77, 112

Hubris, 76–77, 105
Humanism, 21, 33, 37–41, 43n
Hume, David, 81
Huntington, Samuel, 76

Identity, 5, 33, 35, 49–52, 55–60, 65, 100, 103, 129, 137, 151
Identity politics, 6, 14, 32, 52
Imagination, 6, 13, 14, 24, 43, 48, 55, 65, 67, 72, 74, 85–86, 95, 100n, 106–7, 110–11, 113, 133n, 162
Immanence, 36–38, 40, 43–44, 57, 88, 135n
Institutions and power, xi–xiv, xix, xx, 3–4, 20–21, 28–29, 93, 117, 123, 129, 131, 133–34, 142, 150, 155, 158, 164
Interdisciplinarity, 2–7
Islam, 33, 38, 46–57, 60n, 163–66

Jacobin imaginary, xvii, 156
Jager, Colin, 45n
Jefferson, Thomas, 137
Judgment, 15–17, 25, 27, 60

Kafka, Franz, 45, 135
Kalyvas, Andreas, 88, 168n
Kant, Immanuel, 15–16, 18–22, 24, 35–36, 38, 44, 56n, 61, 115, 133n, 139
Klimis, Sophie, 10n, 157n

La Boétie, Étienne, 136, 142, 161–62, 176
Law, 20, 32, 44–45, 57, 59, 71, 81, 93–94, 110, 114–15, 118–19, 129, 134, 137, 144, 152, 157, 159, 164n, 176, 178–79; of God, 32, 45, 119; and lawlessness, 154n, 155, 178–79; and legality, 15, 60, 117, 152, 158, 178; and legislation, 79, 152, 157, 179; metaphysics of, 45, 119

Lee, Peggy, 43
Lefort, Claude, 120–44
Liberalism, xvii, 44, 46–48, 134,
    144, 147–50, 158, 164, 170,
    172–74, 180
Living being, 24, 82, 85, 87, 91,
    94–106
Luxemburg, Rosa, 44, 157
Lyotard, Jean-François, 147

Machiavelli, Niccolò, 128, 142–43
Mahmood, Saba, 14n, 31, 46–61
Makdisi, George, 38
March, Andrew, 58n
Marx, Karl, 58, 152
Marxism, 10, 157
Maturana, Humberto, 95–99,
    114, 115
McClure, Kirstie, 86
Merleau-Ponty, Maurice, 123, 128
Michelet, Jules, 126n, 139
Miracle, 79–83
Mitchell, W.J.T., 54–55
Modernity, 7–10, 18, 23, 27, 33, 36,
    40, 42, 62, 82, 118, 121–22,
    125–33, 136, 138–42, 177
Monotheism, 35, 59, 63, 67, 82, 84,
    127, 130
Montaigne, Michel de, 143
Morality, 8, 20, 28, 36, 41–42, 59,
    70, 74, 88, 169n
Mufti, Aamir, xvi, 9n, 31n
Myth, xiii, 26, 72–73, 79, 82, 103–5,
    108, 135, 169n

Nation, 118, 119, 124, 129, 159, 168–69,
    175; nation-state, xx, 153, 162, 168,
    176; national economy, 148–49,
    153, 168–69, 173; nationalism, 31,
    52, 119, 129, 165, 170–71, 175
Negri, Antonio, 177
Nietzsche, Friedrich, 23, 38, 38n, 69,
    72–73

Nomos, 70–71, 91, 94, 103, 105–6,
    108, 117, 119, 129
Norms, 84, 86–87, 129, 131, 149; and
    the abnormal, 99; and
    normalization, 41, 86; and
    normativity, 31–32, 46–48, 50,
    86–87

Obama, Barack, 33n, 144n
Orientalism, 12, 53, 164, 166, 169n,
    170
Otherness, 8, 42–45, 70, 72, 92,
    94, 102–3, 110, 115–17, 129–30,
    159, 179

Paine, Thomas, 87
Panourgia, Neni, 168n
Parrhēsia, 18–19
Pascal, Blaise, 73–74
Pedagogy, xii–xv, 3–5, 83, 99, 167,
    176, 179
Performativity, xiii, 11, 69, 74, 76,
    78, 118, 127, 132
Perloff, Marjorie, 2, 6–7
Philosophy, xvii, 2, 9–10, 37–38n,
    42, 70, 75–76, 81–82, 108, 128,
    137, 140
Physis, 79–80, 85, 91, 94, 103, 105–6,
    108
Pindar, 71
Plato, 8–9, 37n, 71, 105
Poetics, 6–7, 10–11, 26, 49–50, 106,
    108, 163
Poiein, 1, 7–13, 24–26, 49, 82, 84,
    103, 115
Poiēsis, xvii, 8–9, 26–27, 108, 116,
    125
Poiētic, 11, 24–25, 27, 67, 94, 102–3,
    106–8, 113, 116–17, 123n, 125, 157
Political, xix, 123–24, 126–28, 133,
    141, 154, 172–74, 180; access to,
    xviii–xx, 151–52; aesthetics of, 10,
    157; deregulation of, 150–54, 174;

and power, 11, 151–52, 154–55, 171, 176–77; and radical imagination, xvii, 14

Political economy, xviii, 148

Political theology, xx, 29, 31, 118, 120–21, 127–28, 137, 138, 141, 165, 177

Politics, xvii, xix–xx, 16, 28, 31, 33, 35, 37, 42, 46, 48–49, 51–52, 76, 97, 117, 123, 127–29, 133, 138, 150, 156–59, 168, 174, 180

Post-secularism, xv, xvii, 65–68, 81, 89, 138–39

Psychoanalysis, 41, 91–92, 94–95, 98, 101–2, 125

Public, xiii, xv–xvi, xix, 2, 4, 8, 12, 80, 143–44, 150, 152, 154, 158–60, 163, 170, 173–75, 177–78, 180

Pussy Riot, 54

Racism, 53, 144n, 171

Religion, 14, 28–29, 32, 34, 39, 41–42, 45, 48–54, 58–59, 61–62, 66, 68, 76, 85, 88, 118, 128, 134, 138–41, 165–66

Revolution, 49, 52, 92, 132–38, 142, 144, 166, 177–79; in Egypt, 160–67, 179; in England, 161; in France, 87, 126n, 139; in Haiti, 166; in Iran, 165

Roger, Philippe, 126n

Rose, Jacqueline, 68

Rousseau, Jean-Jacques, 137

Sacred, 44, 49, 52, 54–56, 58, 61, 68, 73, 117–19, 121, 130

Said, Edward, xv, 10, 11n, 12–13, 22, 53, 63, 83, 84n

Sappho, 112

Sartre, Jean-Paul, 94

Saussure, Ferdinand de, xiii

Scalia, Antonin, 80–82

Schmitt, Carl, 29, 82, 120, 134, 137, 138–39

Secular, xvi–xviii, xx, 24–25, 46, 48, 61, 66–67, 139, 162, 165–66; authorization of, 39; detranscendentalizing of, 14, 28–31, 37, 64, 67; as theological, 14–15; 29, 32, 34, 63, 67–68

Secular criticism, 25, 28–30, 63–64, 67–68, 121; as practice, xiv–xv, xvii, 13, 22, 62; as task, 12–13, 46, 64, 68

Secularism, xv, xvii, xx, 1, 12, 14–15, 28–32, 34, 36, 46–48, 51, 53–54, 60–61, 63–65, 67–68, 119, 120–21, 139, 165

Secularization, 23, 29–30, 32–34, 39, 65–67, 126, 134, 139–40

Self-alteration, 11, 18, 36, 40, 44–45, 92, 103, 115

Self-determination, 10, 49–51, 100–101, 106, 110, 114, 136, 159–60, 162, 165, 168, 175–76

Self-interrogation, xiii, 4–6, 13, 17, 19–20, 25, 40, 56n, 60n, 68, 83

Self-limitation, 86

Sexuality, 43n, 50, 171; and sexual difference, 18n, 50–51, 131

Skepticism, xii, xvii, 13, 20, 22–24, 83–84, 110

Smith, Adam, 150

Social-imaginary, 9, 29–30, 34, 39–40, 44, 49, 66–67, 69, 71, 88–89, 102–5, 107, 111, 124–25, 128, 131–32, 140, 142, 150, 166–67

Socrates, 37–38n, 71, 75

Sophocles, xix, 71, 86, 157

Sovereignty, xii–xv, xx, 17–18, 82, 116, 132, 137, 152, 155, 169, 171–73, 177

Spinoza, Baruch, 38, 81, 120, 143

Spivak, Gayatri Chakravorty, 1

Taylor, Charles, 36–45, 88
Technology, 2, 5n, 9, 21, 46, 116, 118,
    163; and media, xvii, xxi, 152, 158,
    174n; and technique, xiv, 9–10,
    21n, 150
Theatricality, xiii, 11, 26–27, 85, 125,
    132, 139, 163
Thiem, Annika, 121n
Tragic sensibility, 23–24, 26–27,
    42–43, 70, 76–78, 85–86, 88,
    104–7, 118
Transcendence, 19, 28, 30, 34–36,
    38–39, 41–43, 46, 49, 64, 69,
    76, 78, 84, 87–88, 105, 113, 115,
    117–19, 128, 132–34, 135n, 139,
    177
Transformation, 6–9, 11, 26, 29–30,
    32–33, 41, 45, 139, 160, 167, 179

Urbinati, Nadia, 173–74

Varela, Francisco, 95–103, 114, 115
Varoufakis, Yanis, 148–49, 173
Vico, Giambattista, 9–10, 11n
Vlastos, Gregory, 79n
Void, 69, 72–73, 126, 130–34,
    136–44, 178

Warner, Michael, xvi, 43n
Weimar, 151, 153, 170
Wittgenstein, Ludwig, 75
Worldliness, 11, 13, 17, 21, 23, 28,
    34–35, 39, 61–63, 74, 77, 80–82,
    84n, 88, 105, 112–13, 126–27, 135,
    143, 165

Žižek, Slavoj, 175, 178n